Taming and Training your Public Speaking Monkeys®

Building Confidence for Public Speaking and Presentations

©Dee Clayton

2012

Suite 321, 17 Holywell Hill, St Albans, Herts. AL1 1DT
Telephone: **01727 537 477** or **01202 798128**
Email: **dee@deeclayton.com**
Website: **www.deeclayton.com**

Published my M-Y Books

187 Ware Road
Hertford
m-ybooks.co.uk

To everyone who wants to or has to stand up and speak

May your message always be heard

Acknowledgements

To mum and dad for your love and continued support always (and for giving me the original wooden monkeys in my 20's!). To my sisters and their families for their continued encouragement and inspiration.

To all my private and corporate clients who have trusted and shared their monkeys with me and gone on to achieve great successes. I'm very proud.

To Kathryn White for starting me on my NLP journey. To David Shephard and all the team at The Performance Partnership including all my fellow NLP'ers who over the last 6 years I've spent many an evening, week or weekend with; learning, practising and coaching. Gerry Murray, Bryce Redford and Susan Cole, it's always a pleasure working with you.

To Karen Moxom for her wonderful work with the Association for NLP CIC – I've always admired her vision in building the UK's largest and most respected organisation for NLP professionals.

To everyone in my business community for their support, referrals, feedback and friendship. Especially Gary Evans for encouraging me to finish this book, Justine Perry for helping my brand live on line and Karen Birch and Katie Steed for their wonderful monkey illustrations.

To M-Y Books and the entire team helping make this a reality.

To everyone else I've met along the way – teachers, colleagues and clients both past and present – sorry if I've not mentioned you by name but thank you for bringing light into my life and to this book.

Last but never least to Leon my loving and supportive partner.

Taming your Public Speaking Monkeys®

Contents

Introduction

If you have a fear of public speaking or are nervous giving presentations I want you to know it's not your fault... It's the fault of your Public Speaking Monkeys® – or, in the visual shorthand I often use to refer to them in this book:

@(O_O)@

These little fellas are a little bit like wild animals running loose inside your mind. They're often out of control and therefore cause you problems. They're the voices in our heads; the ones responsible for last-minute presentation nerves, acute anxiety and the fear of public speaking. You know the ones don't you? They whisper or perhaps even roar discouraging and often negative remarks; the voices say familiar things like:

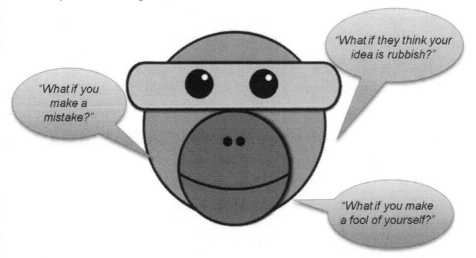

"What if they think your idea is rubbish?"

"What if you make a mistake?"

"What if you make a fool of yourself?"

Doubt

More often than not the monkey voices are negative internal voices that put doubt in your mind about your presenting abilities. Perhaps you find the anxiety sometimes stops you even trying to get up to speak – so you miss opportunities. The result could be a missed promotion, a lost sale or just that frustrating feeling of not getting your views heard.

Discouragement

These voices then ultimately discourage you from talking in front of others altogether. People often look for ways to avoid talking. They even become quite creative in their excuses to avoid it – feigning a sore throat, pulling a sickie or plain refusing to speak. Those affected like this are always the last to volunteer.

Worry

One of the most destructive problems with the negative voices or @(O_O)@ is that we can build up anticipation further... So we spend more time thinking about the worry than preparing.

With all the stress and strain your mind goes blank; you may become panic-stricken and lose the ability to think straight. Your mind becomes a muddle or goes totally blank.

People often tell me about a feeling of inadequacy or a fear of looking weak to colleagues or in front of customers or the boss. Perhaps you are the boss and know that everyone's looking at you – expecting you to perform, to motivate, to inspire but instead you come out with the same old quarterly review slides and begin the slow, painful "death by PowerPoint®" routine.

If you spend more time worrying than practising or you just know how much this problem is holding you back then now's the time to act!

The aim of this book is to work with you every step of the way so that together we can tame those wild animals. In the first part of the book you'll begin to gain control over the monkey voices and tame and befriend them. It may seem a little way off yet, but once they're on your side they can actually be very helpful. Taming the monkeys and getting them on your side is the most important part of losing your fears and becoming a calm more relaxed speaker.

The second part of this book then starts to begin the process of training the @(O_O)@ – it shows you how to ask them to work with you so that you can

> **Taming the monkeys and getting them on your side is the most important part of losing your fears and becoming a calm more relaxed speaker**

be a confident and good speaker. I share a huge selection of tips and tricks that have worked for my clients for many years – and these new approaches and techniques can only be learnt, absorbed and used after the monkeys have been tamed.

When you take some time to understand the process and follow the instructions this programme will work for you. The only caveat is that this process isn't designed to address a genuine medical phobia of public speaking. There are NLP (Neuro Linguistic Programming) techniques designed specifically to rid people of their phobias and this isn't one of them – for more information please contact me directly.

— Dee@DeeClayton.com.

A little bit about the author

Research has shown that the very thought of speaking in public – or even presenting to a small and familiar audience such as your sales team – can generate feelings of intense anxiety. But what if standing up and speaking to an audience is an essential part of your job or business? Dee Clayton has designed and developed her own proven multi-award-winning techniques to transform the nervous, hesitant or just plain boring presenter into a confident speaker who understands how to truly engage an audience and share their key messages for lasting impact.

Dee has spoken in front of tens of thousands of people in all sorts of different situations over the last 24 years.

Dee's background is in business management and marketing; a career that began auspiciously when she had the honour of being awarded The Cooperative Prize for Best Marketing Student. She graduated in Business Studies with Marketing, has a CIM (Chartered Institute of Marketing) Diploma in Marketing and is now a professional member of the CIM. She went on to win the Director's Award 2001 for her work on Boddingtons beer.

Having worked on a wide range of products for brands as diverse as Bernard Matthews, Jacob's Creek, Pizza Hut and Jammie Dodgers to name a few, Dee understands how challenging it can be to get your message across to others in a way that makes them want to buy your product or service or share your passion.

Fascinated with all areas of "communications", Dee is always eager to develop her own skills. In fact, over the last four years alone (alongside developing two businesses) she has invested over 2,400 hours in her own growth and development, thereby ensuring she continues to add value to every project and everybody she shares with.

If four years sounds like a long time, you'll be pleased to know that you can learn much faster with Dee's help – because she's passionate about a technique called Neuro Linguistic Programming (don't let the name put you off!). Not only is she a Trainer and Master Practitioner of NLP – she's also the Marketing Director for the Association of NLP (ANLP). Dee uses her

NLP skills to "model" or copy the best practice and key elements from excellent speakers such as Barack Obama. She combines this with proven NLP techniques as well as her own successes (and "failures"!). Dee then blends all this together with her unique multi-award-winning Public Speaking Monkeys® approach so that you can eliminate any fears and quickly learn best practice tips and tricks to help you achieve success in public speaking. And because Dee's invested those four long years in learning the NLP ropes, you don't need to! Instead, you can use Dee's experience and expertise to fast-track your learning!

To develop her own speaking ability, Dee took every opportunity to get on her feet and learn the skills of great communicators. In addition to formal training , throughout her career she's put herself forward for a huge variety of speaking situations – ITN & BBC TV news interviews, debating wine vintages in Australia, teaching NLP in India and even doing stand-up comedy gigs in Camden! The purpose of the comedy was twofold – to push her own comfort levels and also to help her bring more humour and fun to her approach because they're such an important part of any learning and change.

Dee Clayton has helped many people just like you to lose their fears and nerves and feel confident. Now she had taken those techniques and condensed them into this book so you can learn to tame your monkeys at your own pace in the comfort of your own home or even on the move.

> *"Before I did Dee's training, I was a confused waffler in front of a large room of people. I definitely had the 'Public Speaking Monkeys' paying me a visit! On Dee's course we went through a 'Taming the Monkeys' process, which was a great balance of fun yet deep learning... Since the training I have presented to networking groups and now believe I am memorable. I actually enjoy it a little bit now! I also feel that I could cope with presenting a seminar much better than I have in the past. I have recommended Dee's course to my colleagues and would definitely recommend it to others."*

Fiona Halsey, Solicitor, NEVES SOLICITORS

> *"Thanks to Dee's approach and training I have the confidence to speak for an hour on most subjects and not allow the "monkeys" to cause mischief."*

David Baum, CEO, DEANEM COLLECTIONS

> *"I really enjoyed the discovery of the monkeys and learning how to deal with them. This is what made your course so different from previous ones that I have attended. Some presentation courses only talk about structure and content; the fact that this one goes deep into our monkeys really makes a difference! Overall it was brilliant! I highly recommend it! BTW, the video*

I was practising for went really well – so much so that they have invited me to present at their global conference! Thanks you for all your help, tips and support!"

Dani Busseni, Category Controller, BEL UK

"I recognised that my fear of speaking and cold calling was having a detrimental effect on my business. My "Monkeys", as Dee calls them, caused sweaty palms, palpitations, shaky voice and the dreaded episodes of blank mind. I would deliver a poor elevator pitch so that few people really grasped what my business was about, I would never speak in public or host an event and would avoid cold calling at all costs. Dee's workshops are fun, action packed and empowering and have successfully tamed those "Monkeys". Thanks to Dee I now enjoy delivering different elevator pitches, have hosted a networking event – and cold calling – and I actually enjoy it! My business has definitely benefited."

Zandra Johnson, Director, FAIRYTALE FURNITURE

"What went really well was learning how to stand still and not need a ream of notes ... I feel completely confident now and I know I will do things differently."

Marion Sambridge, Director, HAWTHORN SOFTWARE SOLUTIONS

"I'd like to thank you very much for the tools you equipped me with....as a result of the things we went through in the first part of the day, I've been warding off those debilitating monkeys and applying myself much better in most other things this week!"

James Newton, Architectural Technologist, NATIVE CHARTERED ARCHITECTS

"Dee is unique in that she would fit all attributes. Thanks to Dee's approach and training I have the confidence to speak for an hour on most subjects and not allow the "monkeys" to cause mischief. Everyone should experience Dee Clayton at work."

Tim Huckle, IT consultant, THINK IT SERVICES

"I met Dee in 2009 but it feels like I've know her forever. Not only is she a warm, engaging and amusing woman, but she adds real value to people's lives. I have seen her help dozens of people improve their confidence when speaking in public.

Many of them are hugely talented and have terrific businesses but the 60 second presentation, a 10 minute PowerPoint gig or that all important sales pitch had become a nightmare for them. Yet after a few hours with Dee they really had turned a corner; not only did their body language, delivery and content improve radically, so did the results.

Monkey is a simple but very smart concept that we can all get our head around; it creates a feeling of camaraderie as we all have them and you can actually feel the room relax as Dee explains how they work their black magic."

June Cory, Owner, MY MUSTARD GOOGLE ADWORDS CONSULTANCY

"Dee helped me to focus on my company presentation skills. I started off in a sea of confusion not knowing what to focus on and Dee navigated me to much calmer waters. Dee helped me conquer my 'doubting monkeys'."

Doug Plunkett, Owner/Massage Therapist, 1LIFE HEALTHCARE

"I used to be petrified and panic a lot when I had to speak in public and I only hosted Business Club once in a while.

Now I am hosting The Business Club on a regular basis as business partner has moved to Australia. My monkeys still pay me a visit but as I start to feel them I come back to calm quickly...

...Recently I even spoke at a rally in Trafalgar square to over 300 people – I would definitely never have done that before!"

Katrina Sargent, Director, THE BUSINESS CLUB WEST HERTS

"... I feel more confident and, now I'm not worrying about the presentation, I can just relax and focus on giving a really good presentation...",

"...Dee I did my presentation yesterday, the one I was preparing for, and it went really well. Your ideas have really worked. Thanks so much for your help."

**Danielle Fagot, Independent Financial Adviser,
RICHMOND HOUSE FINANCIAL SERVICES**

Dee's "bigger picture" vision is to enable people to become better communicators, whatever their message may be. She has seen plenty of good ideas out there and is sure there are many more; but they often fail to see the light of day due to poor communications. Dee knows from her 21 years in marketing that a good idea is worth nothing if you can't inspire other people to come with you, to follow you, to believe in your idea, product or vision.

Dee likes to believe that if we want to improve the world in which we live then leaders, business people, fund raisers, inventors and people from all walks of life need to be able to communicate their ideas with passion and clarity. She wonders what would happen if we could all communicate better and understand one another's point of view more quickly and easily. Wouldn't we find solutions more easily? With all the intelligence and facilities available to us today it can't be just the science or technology that stands in our way – but also our human beliefs and behaviours.

The world needs more people to be able to communicate their ideas effectively; it needs people to overcome their fears and share their message; people like you to stand up and play your part, however large or small.

A journey of a thousand miles begins with a single step.

Lao-tzu, The Way of Lao-tzu, Chinese philosopher (604 BC – 531 BC)

Overview

Before we get on with the specifics I want to take you briefly through the book outline chapter by chapter. Most people read the book from front to back – and that's strongly recommended because in each chapter there's information that will help you in the next. However some people, perhaps, who've already done a lot of self development or other techniques around self awareness, may already have a good knowledge of some of the ideas I'm sharing in this book. They might just want to skim read some of the sections and then go into others in more depth. So let me share with you briefly what to expect from this Taming the Monkeys programme.

In this first chapter you'll get to see why the @(O_O)@ are a problem and how they can send you on a downward negative spiral. To set you up for success I ask you to express what you personally want to achieve from this programme. In Chapter 2 we learn a little more about the monkeys: their traits and the impact they have upon you. This will give you insights into why this unique multi-award-winning approach, while probably different from anything you've experienced before, will work when you follow the instructions fully.

In Chapter 3 we go into a little more detail about changing your mindset because, as you'll discover, these @(O_O)@ are all in the mind. We often like to think we know how to change our mind but more often than not we aren't clear on how to make the changes stick over the long term. Have you ever made a New Year's resolution? Have you perhaps stuck to it for an hour, day or month, but eventually just gone back to how you used to be? This book helps you to lose your fear and change your attitude towards speaking **forever**. And in order to make permanent changes you need to know the secret ingredients for positive, permanent change.

In the next chapter, 4, I share with you a bird's eye view of the Taming the Monkeys technique, showing you step by step how the process works, using a typical client example. In a live training session I'd give a demonstration of how the exercise works before asking you to complete it – so this is in effect the live demo section! As we go through and tame "Georgie's" monkeys you'll get an idea of how the process works. We also cover a few key approaches that show you both what to do and what to watch out for. @(O_O)@ are clever and very mischievous – they have plenty of tricks up their sleeves to try and throw you off track. As a professional monkey trainer I've seen all these tricks before so I warn you about them in advance in order to recognise them and avoid them. Because of this trickery, I also recommend that you have a "monkey buddy" – someone to support you through the process – and Chapter 4 offers recommendations and guidance on who to choose and what they need to do. There's even a note you can show them so they don't have to read the whole book!

Chapter 5 is the "live" chapter. This is where you get to complete the Taming the Monkeys process. I explain why it's important that once you start the process you don't stop (except for comfort breaks of course!) So it's important to read the preparation sections before completing this chapter to help you sail smoothly through the exercises, avoiding the monkey's traps along the way. Because these are powerful techniques there are a couple of warnings that run alongside these, so please take notice and only go ahead if it's safe for you to do so.

Now that you've tamed your personal @(O_O)@ it's the right time to learn some new skills. But beware – this is unlikely to work if you haven't tamed your monkeys yet so make sure you've done this first. Chapter 6 introduces you to the most helpful attitudes to have from a mindset point of view. After all, until now your mind has been full of negative monkey chatter and there is now space to introduce some more helpful, positive monkey attitudes so you can continue on the upward spiral of speaking success. We also cover some of the basics for understanding and developing successful body language that will help you to maintain the best frame of mind.

In Chapter 7 we cover some tips and techniques on structuring your content and how to prepare and practice for your presentation or talk. There are many ways in which you can approach these things and these are some of the best and simplest ways I've come across so far.

Chapter 8 gives a few pointers on approaching and delivering the talk on the day, including my views on PowerPoint®. We also talk about the value of now being able to hear feedback in a balanced and helpful manner instead of having it tainted, often in a more negative light by those pesky monkeys.

In Chapter 9 I really encourage you to do some thinking about what you now want to achieve from your speaking. Instead of settling for being an OK speaker, do you want to grow and develop in order to help you to achieve greater things? Who knows, probably you don't even know yet because you haven't tamed the @(O_O)@ but, trust me, once you have you'll be able to think about the future and all those things you've always wanted to do but felt held back before. The process I take you through is very thorough and detailed for a reason – I know it works!

In the final chapter, 10, we pull together the thoughts and learning from the previous chapters and I share my thoughts about "finding your inner speaker". We also take a look at your next steps, should you want to keep moving forward. Because speaking well is often seen as a journey, not a destination, I give you a few tips on where to go next and what additional programmes I offer too.

The process I'm going to take you through later is a little different. Well I guess you'd want it to be, right? Because whatever you've tried before hasn't worked properly or you wouldn't be reading this book would you? (Unless you're just curious about it – or you know me and thought you'd better buy the book! Thanks Mum and Dad!). You're probably reading this book because you're suffering from a fear or worry about public speaking in some way. It may be that the nerves are so bad you just avoid any speaking, or perhaps you get on and speak anyway knowing your fears and concerns are adversely affecting your performance. Whatever your reason for reading, you're in the right place.

Whether you've been on presentation skills courses or read books on the topic many times before, or this is your first journey into overcoming your fears, this technique is the one that will work for you... forever. It will provide you with a long-term solution to overcoming your speaking fears, nerves and anxieties. It's already worked for thousands of people and that's why it's won so many innovation awards – because it's a fresh approach *that works*. It's worked for others so it will work for you. All you need to do is follow the simple steps with an open mind.

Taming your Public Speaking Monkeys®
Chapter 1 –
Monkey spirals

In this first chapter you'll begin to get a feel for what monkeys can say and why they're a problem, sending you on a negative downward spiral. Becoming a confident speaker is all about being on an upward spiral which starts with understanding that there's a problem and then getting in touch with what result you personally want from doing this programme.

Examples of monkey voices

You may think you are the only one with negative @(O_O)@ voices muttering away in your head, but believe me they're more common than you think. And, having worked with many thousands of people and their monkeys, I want to share with you below some of the most common things that people's @(O_O)@ say. That doesn't mean they're all there for the same reason, and we'll talk more about that in later chapters, but for now take a look through this list and see which, if any, of these resonate with you.

"You're going to get tongue tied!"

You're going to...	What if you...
o Visibly shake or show your nervousness	o Open your mouth and nothing comes out
o Forget what you want to say	o Are incoherent
o Freeze, faint or cry	o Bore them to tears
o Get tongue tied	o Get interrupted
o Blush or get really sweaty	o Get asked an expected question
o Trip over your words	o Read from your script
o Talk too fast or speak too quickly	o Are afraid you're not interesting enough
o Lose your notes or forget your place	o Aren't prepared enough.
o Get really nervous	o Get the numbers wrong
o Rush through things so the presentation is over quickly	o Make errors in the presentation
o Get embarrassed standing up	o Suffer technology failure
o Be the focus of attention and stared at	o Lose your train of thought
o Get nervous before and while presenting.	o Can't keep the audience interested
o Hate everyone looking at you	o Have a wavering voice and croak
o Forget what you're saying	o Haven't practised enough
o Be too detailed and not be concise enough in the time	o Lose track of the structure
o Feel physically sick	o Feel that everyone is "checking me out" and judging you
o Feel your heart beat really fast	o Don't get your message across
o Get your words muddled up	o Can't answer a question on the spot
o Mess up	o Appear really boring
o Go red around the neck	o Feel conscious because of your weight
o Get asked something you don't know	o Aren't liked by the audience
o Make a mistake	o Not good enough
o Sound rubbish	o Can't do it
o Speak too quietly	o Dry up
	o Talk rubbish

Monkey spirals

You can't opt out of the monkey spirals or the @(O_O)@ – they'll either work with you or against you. Either the voices will be saying negative, discouraging remarks, or positive, helpful remarks – you can't be monkey neutral. If you don't train the little fellas they'll work against you and make your performance worse. But when you start to get the Public Speaking Monkeys® under control and working on your side, the good news is you can't help but improve on your results. Let me explain.

Unfortunately, a lot of people seem to be on the monkey downward spiral. They hear the monkey voices and begin to dread speaking so they start to feel fearful they talk about it with their friends who fuel or feed their monkey fears or they totally ignore the monkeys and hope they'll go away. The physical conditions start to kick in and as you start to sweat you feel more nervous. As you get up to speak, your hands are shaking so you drop your notes, making you even more flustered. Your mouth's dry so you take a sip of water but your shaking hands spill a little on your notes and create an embarrassing spot on the new suit you'd bought especially for today. Because of your panic, you forget to turn off your phone which rings as you mutter your first words. Oh well, at least it gets the attention of the room! You become short of breath, speak more quietly, back away from the audience and start to gabble quickly to get it all over and done with. This is just the beginning of the downward spiral because next time you'll recall every last minute in painful detail!

Part of the reason that fear is such a debilitating emotion when it's out of proportion is that it can feel so bad that it prevents you from trying things. Once you get the @(O_O)@ under control and working for you, even if only a little bit at first, you'll find it so much easier to keep going, to work through any less positive emotions, knowing that there's something brighter on the other side.

On top of the internal stuff, the monkeys affect your audience too. If you're feeling nervous and full of @(O_O)@ when you present, then I know you'll be performing below par because you'll be too worried about what's going on inside your head to give much thought to the audience. You aren't thinking about how they're reacting and what you might need to do to connect more or build more rapport with them. You aren't looking to see if you need to explain things a little more clearly, motivate them into action or any other such objectives for your talk or presentation.

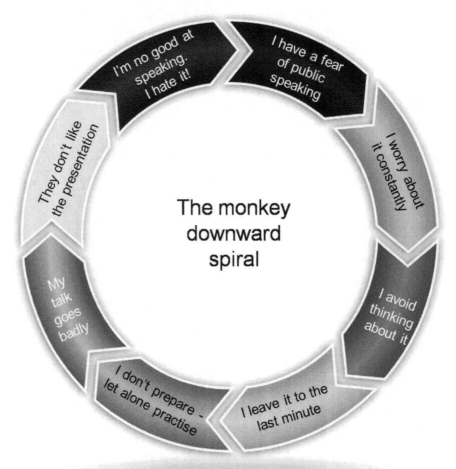

Figure 1 – Negative thinking – the monkey downward spiral

I want to show you how you can be your best and share your message in a manner that will help you to achieve what you want, and that begins with learning to travel on the upward spiral. This begins when you take the first step to taming your monkeys and work with them, not against them. You'll recognise them and know how to manage them and become calmer and more relaxed about speaking.

The reason taming the monkeys is such a critical first step to speaking success is because it's the key to moving your thoughts from a negative downward spiral to a positive upward spiral. As you move through this programme you'll start to see and experience mini successes, which in turn make you feel better and more confident. Will everything be totally perfect? Probably not – but as your negative @(O_O)@ diminish they take less of your focus and time. You begin to see that the focus needs to be outside yourself – with the audience; not with you inside your head. So naturally you start to please the audience more. They don't really care if you get all your words perfectly right but they do care whether you're interesting *to* them and *INTERESTED IN THEM*. So decide now that you want the @(O_O)@ to work with you and not against you.

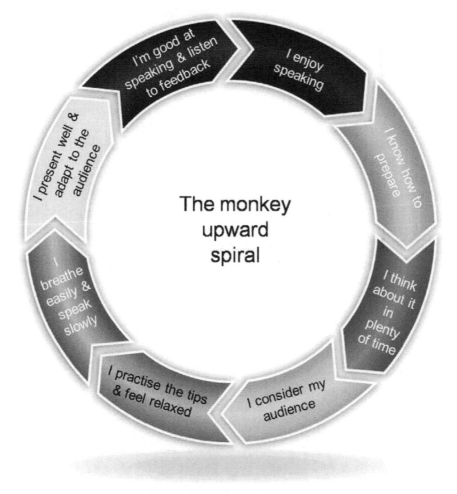

As you become more relaxed you'll be better able to breathe more easily, get more oxygen to the brain and think on your feet. Your body language will improve and you'll automatically stand taller. As you stand taller, your head will become more upright and you'll be confident enough to try new techniques, engage with the audience and begin to make eye contact. The audience will respond more positively and the energy in the room will pick up. You'll feel the energy and confidence pick up and become even more relaxed, so the audience relaxes and really starts connecting with you and the message you're *sharing.*

The four keys to switching spirals

The four keys to switching spirals looks at what elements make up long-term successful change. I don't want you to switch to the upward spiral just temporarily; I want you to know how to do it forever and to do that you need these four keys.

The process of successfully changing from a fearful speaker to a confident one requires four key elements, which we work through in this book.

1) **Acknowledge why this is important to you – what are you missing out on or what do you want?** Your fear of speaking might mean you're lacking the confidence you want, missing additional sales or being overlooked for promotion. Perhaps you're losing sleep before a presentation or want to advance your skills. The Public Speaking Monkeys, when left to run wild, are a problem, preventing you from having what you deserve. These early chapters are about laying solid foundations so the next step of monkey taming can take place. You don't want to build a house on dodgy foundations – it won't last long. To go through this process effectively you mustn't miss out anything – but by reading this book you're already well on the way to resolving the problem because you've overcome the first hurdle – *knowing there's a problem.* The next exercise helps you to look at the problem in a little more depth – a bit like doing a house survey before you start work on improving it!

2) **Focusing on what you *do* want**. Because the monkeys have been chattering negatively in your head, it's all too easy for us to think about what we don't want. In order to change your public speaking mindset permanently you need to focus on what you *do* want, not what you *don't want*. Next there are a few questions to identify what you do want from this programme, and at the end of the book there's a section dedicated to focusing on what you want achieve in the future with your new skills and positive frame of mind (but that may seem a way off yet!). Once you've done this you're ready to neutralise the negatives. Knowing what you want and what you're aiming for will help you to have the energy to see you past any small challenges when neutralising those negatives or help you try new things.

3) **Finding and neutralising negative feelings.** Whether you realise it or not there are likely to be some negative feelings or thoughts lurking behind this fear of speaking that might not be immediately visible. They're a bit like a bad smell. You know there is one but perhaps you don't know quite where it's coming from and you certainly might not know how smelly it really is until you go outside in the fresh air. Only then might you realise the impact the problem is having upon you and how genuinely keen you are to be rid of it. In order to eliminate the smell, you need to uncover what's causing it and where it's coming from so that you can neutralise it. The unique Taming the Monkeys process covered in these earlier chapters takes you step by step through examples and exercises that enable you to uncover where the bad feelings and thoughts around speaking are coming from. That way you can neutralise them and get the @(O_O)@ working on your side.

By doing this, you'll get rid of the fear. You'll learn to respond in different and better ways to the *idea* of public speaking and only then can you open your mind and adopt the practical techniques and speaking approaches covered in the Training your Monkeys section from Chapter 6 onwards. Too many people try to get rid of their fear by going directly to the skills section; by learning new things, but this is only effective once you've tamed the monkeys. Otherwise it's like covering the bad smell with an air freshener: it's a temporary fix but the smell will soon return once the 30 days of pine freshness are up!

4) **Take action to improve your mindset, skills and habits.** The final piece in the "monkey puzzle" comes after you've neutralised your fear of speaking in order to learn some good approaches to stand you in good stead. No longer being scared, in itself, will not make you a good speaker – it will just make you a "not scared" speaker. Speaking is a skill like many other things, and the best mindset, attitudes and skills for public speaking and presenting need to be learnt and practiced. This section is all about the first steps in training your monkeys to be on your side. Once the fear's have been neutralised you'll notice how much easier it is to take on board new approaches and skills. Of course in this book we can't cover everything to do with becoming an excellent speaker but I've summarised and included some of the most common questions, challenges and useful tips from years of personal experience and client questions.

"*Don't read on – you'll never be a good speaker!*"

What do you want to achieve?

Let's take a quick look at the first and second keys – identifying where you are now in your speaking journey and where you want to be in the future after finishing this book. At this point many people say, "its simple – I have a fear of presenting and want to get rid of it" and yes, that's the big picture problem. And what you need to do in order to make the process work is to pull that thought apart a little more and understand the problem in more detail. Once that's done we'll work together through what it is you WANT (not DON'T WANT!).

Log book

With any journey it's important to keep notes to which you can refer at any time. Write your findings and learning down as you move through exercises from this book. Use a public speaking workbook big enough to use in the future for feedback from your talks, not only for this leg of the journey. Those who track and recognise their speedy progress always get the best results. If you're already speaking in public, you'll want to take your workbook with you everywhere – you never know when a new goal idea might pop up or when an unruly monkey might start muttering and you need to write down what they're saying.

Understanding your starting point

When you start any journey it's important to know where you're starting from. Have you ever programmed in a new destination into your navigation system only to find it hasn't yet updated your current location? It gives you all the wrong information – tells you to turn the wrong way and makes you think it will take ages to get there. Only once the system connects with the GPS does it start to get a more sensible and accurate reading of your current location. If you don't do this exercise you will have easily overcome your fears by the end of the book – but you might not remember how bad it was to begin with (where you started from). The problem with that is that you might not believe that you know how to make the journey on your own in the future. It's tricky to be confident of the route you took if you don't remember the starting point. Self-belief and confidence in knowing the process are essential ingredients in achieving long term success rather than a flash in the pan solution – so please do follow these instructions now.

Exercise – measuring your current location

 We want to measure how you feel now – *before* starting the taming process. Imagine how you feel when you're really experiencing the fear of speaking in public or giving a presentation. Imagine you're just about to go on stage and stand up in front of lots of people.

As you picture this, rate how you feel on a confidence scale of 1 – 10 where 1 = no confidence at all and terrified and 10 = very confident, relaxed and looking forward to the presentation.

If you haven't presented yet, just imagine how you'd feel.

Write your answer down in your workbook. Good. Now we have a measure of where you're starting from.

Your reasons for reading this book

As mentioned, these early chapters are about laying solid foundations so the next step of monkey taming can take place. There are some key questions that will help you to uncover your inner thoughts and feelings about public speaking. I'll take you through the specific questions one by one first so that you understand them and also give you some examples of previous answers so you can see you're heading along the right lines.

After that there's an exercise for you to go ahead and spend some time completing yourself. This section is only about what you want from "this" programme so keep it programme-specific. At the end of the book there's a goal-setting section for your more general speaking goals – so that's where you should plan for the future.

It's important to plan what we want from this book, otherwise when we finish it we won't know whether or not we've achieved what we set out to achieve. Part of success is seeing and recognising what you've achieved as well as what can be improved. Unfortunately the monkeys may prevent you from seeing success, so we're going to practice recognising how we're doing as we progress.

a) *"What is it you want?"*

The answer to this question needs to be stated in a positive way and in as much detail as possible. Many clients I work with when we do this exercise begin to realise that they need to spend time to get to know what it is they actually want. This may seem like an odd statement at first, but most people are only very sure what they *don't* want. When I ask people who are starting out on their programmes what they want, they say things like, "I don't want to be nervous", "I don't want to flap my hands about", "I don't want to speak too quickly" or "I don't want to mess it up like last time". The problem with this is that our inner mind struggles to understand fully a comment phrased in a negative way. For example if you say, "I don't want to feel sick", your inner mind has to be thinking about feeling sick in order to process the sentence. So then you unintentionally end up with an image of feeling sick in your head. In fact, that's so true I'm going to have to stop thinking about it now!

In order to focus on what you do want you may write:

"At the team meeting next month I want to feel calm, confident and relaxed when I give my monthly update presentation. I want to be well prepared, feel confident that I know my key points and to be relaxed enough to be listening fully to questions when they're asked."

Some people are really clear on what they want from the programme and others need to spend time considering what they want before they really know. It's an ongoing process so, as you learn more about yourself, you might want to refine your answers as you move through the book. The most important thing is to have recorded these answers so you can refer back to them and see how far you've travelled and progressed along the way.

Tip: Many find it easier to say what they **don't want** rather than what they do, so it might be easier to answer question b) first and then come back and answer question a) with the opposites.

b) *"What is happening now?"*

This question is asking about the current situation – so you might write about what's happening now, how you feel about that and what you think and say about it either to yourself or others. For example

"Currently at the team meetings I'm nervous and worried about presenting; I hate it – and I know I go red when I stand up. I never have enough time to prepare properly and I lose my thread as I'm speaking. When it comes to the questions at the end, I dread someone asking me something I can't answer. I tell myself to hurry through the presentation as quickly as possible so I can sit back down!"

c) **"What will you see, hear and feel when you have it?"**

In this next question you need to imagine you've got what you want; that you've achieved it already. The best thing to do is to role-play a little and make this image something you really want, to make the image really compelling. Imagine being there in the future and looking around you – what do you see? What do you hear and what do you feel?

You may think that you want to be confident so surely you can skip the rest of this exercise...but it is important you know what "confidence" means to you. Is it a feeling? How much of it do you want? How would you know you had it?

You might imagine "well prepared, confident and relaxed" as the following scenario:

You turn up early, having checked the room layout, already safe in the knowledge that it's all set up as you wanted it to be. You know the technology works because you tested it and you know you have everything you need because you've checked all your hand-outs. You now have time to mingle with people before the team meeting. You feel calm and relaxed and engage the people confidently in conversation. You're listening to what's said and responding appropriately because you're calm and relaxed. They tell you how much they're looking forward to hearing your plans and ideas in the meeting later.

When the time for your bit comes along, you stand up and as you look around you see a sea of warm, friendly faces. People are looking forward to what you have to say.

As you glide through your presentation, you eloquently make your points and guide the audience through a well-structured presentation. They nod and agree with you on your key points. At the end of your session, you wrap up with a clear and concise summary, knowing you've made your point clearly and influenced others to consider the content. As you finish, they ask questions that you can easily answer and that you enjoy answering. Their questions mean they're as passionate and interested in the topic as you are.

You know it's gone well and all your colleagues tell you how well you did. It feels great – you feel relaxed and confident. Best of all, you recorded your presentation yourself so you can listen back to it in due course and really appreciate what went well – after all, when you're in the presentation flow you don't always consciously remember everything that was said, you just know it went well.

d) "How will you know when you have what you want?"

What evidence will you have to tell you that you've been successful? What will you see, hear, feel and know when you have it specifically?

This question is in place to encourage you to have clear criteria so you know when you've achieved your aims. Often, people don't realise how far they've travelled because they've never said what "success" looks like. This question's slightly different from the one above because it's asking for evidence. For example, feedback forms have their strengths and weaknesses but, when well designed, can be a good measure for success. I set myself targets on participant results and also the percentage of people who are happy to refer me, because I see that as a significant measure of success.

Your own evidence might be getting a good night's sleep the day before, someone saying something or taking a specific action that you asked them to. Spend time thinking about how you could measure your success. Remember that if you aren't presenting during the time you're reading this book you'll need to set yourself a realistic measure so that you'll know you've achieved it even without doing a speech. For example, when I think about presenting I remain calm and consider how best to structure it.

e) "What will having this result or outcome do for you?" When you achieve your outcome what will having it allow you to do and/or have?

As with all these questions, you need to answer from your gut feeling – whatever comes to mind. For example, "I'll feel happy and confident, I'll be able to relax and sleep better before presentations, I'll be able to be considered for promotion and begin to investigate my new business idea or I'll be able to feel confident in my own mind about the thought of presenting".

f) "Can you start and maintain this yourself?" Is this outcome self-initiated

and can it be self-maintained?

The aim of this question is to ensure that you're totally responsible for what you want to achieve and not relying on others to do it for you. It's good to ask others to help but not to abdicate responsibility for your own results. What you will find is that only when you take 100% responsibility for your results will others help you to achieve them. The answer will probably be yes – or if it's no, you need to re-word what you want or find another way to ensure this is 100% your responsibility, which might include regular updates with anyone you've allocated tasks to.

g) *"In what context do you want this?" Where, when, how and with whom does this result or outcome apply?*

This question just allows you to consider the different environments and contexts in which you speak or think about speaking. Your goal might initially be about work, but when you think about it perhaps you'll also want to use your skills to help promote a local charity or to follow a hobby you've not been confident enough to consider before. Perhaps the context is in your front room... Once you've completed the book and all the exercises, how will you be feeling?

h) *"What do you need to do this?" What help is needed to get your outcome? Are the resources internal or external? In other words, do you have what you need or do you need resources from elsewhere? What needs to be done to get the help you need?*

This question is designed to identify what you need in order to be successful – and this programme is a great start. Alone, it is not enough though. You need time, for example, to complete the exercises as well as motivation and perhaps some support. I talk about Monkey Buddies later and strongly recommend that you find one. There may be other things you need to do in order to ensure you have everything you need to be successful – better to know about it now so you can go ahead and work on gathering everything you need.

i) *"Does this fit with your worldview and ethics?"*

1. **What will you gain and lose when you have your outcome?**

2. **Does this fit in comfortably with all the other areas of your life?**

3. What impact will this have on other people in your life?

These sub-questions help to pick out some specifics to ensure that the programme is totally in alignment with who you are and what you want to achieve. Some people, for example, might be aiming to spend more time with their children and think that by spending time on this programme they're spending less time with their children. That might well be the case in the short term – but on the other hand, by breaking the pattern of fear, they can spend less time in the future over preparing or worrying and instead spend more quality time with their family if they choose. They will also benefit by ensuring they don't pass on their fear of speaking to their kids. Some clients even choose to do this programme with their children so it becomes a joint activity and benefits everyone! Only you can know what's right for you and there's no point going forward until you're happy with the answers to the questions above. If there are any clashes, just think them through and adjust your approach until you're happy with it. Now I've shared with you how to go about answering these questions it's your turn to do a little work!

Exercise – laying the foundations

1. Consider questions a)to i) above and write both the questions and answers down in your workbook

2. If you need to just guess at the answers, go ahead – it will still work!

3. Write down all your answers however silly they may seem.

4. Don't over analyse this exercise – just run with it and see what comes up. Go with the flow!

Warning:

If you don't track your progress in writing you might receive a visit from the "I'm not progressing fast enough" monkey or the "I'm not doing this right so I'd better stop halfway through the programme" monkey!

When you do write everything in your workbook you'll be able to:

➢ Easily see your progress

➢ Remind yourself of any key learning

➢ Update your findings as you go along.

Key takeaways

✓ Monkey spirals can only work for or against you – there is no neutral no man's land. This book and its techniques are all about giving you the mindset to start on the upward spiral and, should you find yourself on the downward spiral, to give you the mindset, tools and techniques to swing yourself quickly across to the upward one.

✓ The process of successfully <u>and permanently</u> changing from a fearful speaker to a confident one requires 4 key elements, which we work through in this book:

    ✓ Acknowledgment that there's an issue that's causing you to miss out or standing in your way

    ✓ Identifying and focusing on what you do want

    ✓ Finding and neutralising negative feelings

    ✓ Take action to improve your mindset, skills and habits

✓ All I ask at this point is that you remain open-minded enough to complete the exercise and allow the answers to come to you as you progress through the programme.

✓ The aim of this programme is to help you to significantly decrease or lose your fear and nerves around presenting. Then you may want to learn and develop into a strong speaker with an important message to share. You might not know what that message is yet, but it may well come to you during the programme.

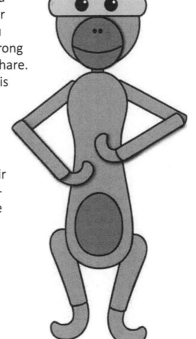

Now you've done some of the foundation-laying you're ready to learn a little more about those cheeky little fellas! Let's take a look at their impact on you and why this unique multi-award-winning approach will work when you follow the programme.

Chapter 2 –
Public Speaking Monkeys®

In this chapter we delve a little deeper into the concept of Public Speaking Monkeys®. We learn a little more about them, what they are and the damage they can cause. We uncover the unpleasant side effects if @(O_O)@ are left untamed, the consequences of feeding the monkeys with more and more negative thoughts and the dangers of trying to ignore them. Having understood all this, you'll be even more committed to taming your monkeys and see why your current situation can no longer continue. We then spend a little time introducing you to the art and science behind the Public Speaking Monkeys® concept, and why this approach works where others may not have.

Behavioural symptoms

This can involve total avoidance of any and all events where speaking in public might be a possibility – often backed up with a cunning list of reasons why for the tenth time your colleague and not you will have to do the talk.

More often, it's a long list of excuses you bring to the audience's attention as you get up to speak – letting them know just how rubbish you really think you are with phrases such as: "I'm not very good at public speaking" or "I hate speaking so if I get a little nervous and flustered do forgive me" or "I hope you don't find this too boring". While this might make you feel better, it's not great for the audience! Now they're not concentrating on what you're saying; they're thinking about how nervous or boring you are because that's what you've drawn attention to and focused their minds on!

ULTIMATELY you won't do your best because of the monkeys inside your head. You'll probably have to give your speech regardless. You won't find it comfortable or enjoy it but at least you'll be able to say you've done it, because you needed to. Phew! Time for a stiff drink!

Physical symptoms

We've talked already about the doubt, discouragement and worry that the @(O_O)@ cause which often has some undesirable side effects:

I'm sure you're well aware of the symptoms people suffer from through fear of speaking: dry mouth, feeling sick, blind panic and butterflies (more like giant bats!), sweaty palms, sweaty face and sweaty armpits (Not the best first impression when you walk on the stage!). No wonder people hide behind the lectern!

Then there's the flushed face, red neck, shaking legs, runny tummy, toilet visits at awkward times, the fainting, inability to sleep and then exhaustion due to lack of sleep! Remind me, why don't you like speaking? Do you have a case of the monkeys?

Why do monkeys give us physical side effects?

Nerves or the feeling of fear is natural and they are there to protect us. If you think of our bodies and minds from an evolutionary standpoint, they're still very much like those of our ancestors in cavemen times. That seems like a long time ago but actually from a developmental point of view it wasn't all that long ago at all.

What this means is that when a threat of any sort is presented to us our bodies will respond with the appropriate hormones. The purpose of fear must naturally be to stop us getting into dangerous situations or to assist us when we do. Some say it is our body's way of telling us to pay attention so we can remain safe. Therefore fear is a helpful emotion – in the right circumstances.

Men and women react differently to stress

Perhaps you've heard of the fight or flight response? Well that tells part of the story, but I've always thought it didn't always accurately reflect *women's* stress response. According to recent research, men and women react differently to stress (Source: *The Tending Instinct: Women, Men and the Biology of Our Relationships.* Shelly E. Taylor, Times Books 2002). This research proposes a new and controversial theory about men and women – one that overturns five decades of stress research but seems intuitively right, and from what I see around me, makes a lot of sense. Make of it what you will.

Until this research, we learnt that when we experience stress it triggers a fight or flight response. Taylor argues a different view using her own and current research. She says that while stress does produce the fight or flight response in men, women respond with a very different cascade of brain chemicals that leads them to reach out to other women and to bond with them. Genius! So this is why we (women) often need to talk about our problems!

Men's fight or flight response

When facing danger, the fight or flight response in men triggers a rush of adrenaline, which provides the body with the resources it needs to respond: either to run or fight.

Taylor argues that it makes evolutionary sense for the male to be ready to fight or run – but not for the female. From an evolutionary point of view, a pregnant female with babies and young children wouldn't increase her family's chances of survival by running. Taylor believes it's more likely that her own survival, and that of her children, would be better served by being part of a large, friendly, female group – as the group itself provides protection. If you look at the behaviour of other primates this is what you see. The females gather in groups and are very successful at defending themselves from danger or the aggressive males in the troupe. From a hormonal point of view, Oxytocin (a primary hormone known for oiling the socialising and networking wheels) plays a large part for women under stress and so a woman can relieve her feelings of anxiety by caring for others.

You may wonder why no one has suggested this theory before. It's because previous studies on the biochemistry of fight or flight mechanisms used only men in the research. Women were often excluded from scientific research studies because it was considered too complicated to allow for our monthly fluctuations in hormones! It is only in the last decade that research on women has been gathered.

The reason I think this is interesting is because previously any solutions that help women reduce stress must have been based on a single stress response for both men and women. I'm hoping that with this additional insight women too can begin to understand their stress responses better and thus manage themselves more effectively. Men can also apply this new knowledge if they want to assist women in stressful situations. Not by assuming they react in the same way as them, but by understanding their need to talk about and around the problem. There is a warning here though for people talking about their problems – YOU MUST NOT UNDER ANY CIRCUMSTANCES BE TEMPTED TO FEED THE MONKEYS.

Women (and men): please don't feed the monkeys

While seeking social support is a good thing and can reduce women's stress levels, in the context of public speaking you must be careful not to feed the @(O_O)@ . I often see it in group training, where people get together and discuss the monkeys. I'm quick to respond and warn people of the dangers of feeding the @(O_O)@ .

A typical monkey feeding conversation might go like this...

I have to present in 10 minutes and I feel so nervous!

I know how you feel. When I speak my mouth goes all dry. Does yours?

Well, umm, let me think about it. I suppose now you mention it yes, my mouth does feel a little dry. Can you pass the water?

Don't drink too much or you might need to go to run off stage to the loo all the time!

Is there time to go to the loo again, do you think?

Yes, but make sure you don't stay in there and get forgotten Ha Ha! Like the lady who fainted every time she did a presentation!

Feeding the monkeys is a process whereby people (often women) spend so long talking and agreeing with one another about how bad their @(O_O)@ are that they actually make them worse, not better.

Be careful not to be a monkey feeder, nor to accept any monkey food!

Applying the science

So applying this to the stress around public speaking it would appear that men are more likely to "get on with it", fight off their monkeys and present anyway even if it's not a comfortable experience (or get a job where they can avoid the situation all together) while women are more likely to seek support among their social networks.

Anecdotally this is a generalised reflection of what I experience from my clients.

Often my male clients have found me through my marketing activity or Google searches. They inquire what services I offer and then make a decision quickly to start the programme. They do their home play, complete the exercises and then are free of their @(O_O)@ and learn the practical skills required for the task in hand. It seems few other people were involved in the decision-making process or even along the way. I guess the males who decide to run away are the ones I don't get to see!

Women, on the other hand, like to talk to others and often come through recommendations from those in their network. They speak to me, often in detail, about the services offered. They take away the marketing materials and then discuss it with peers or partners before deciding to work with me. Unlike men, women seem to go through the programme in consultation with others, perhaps talking to friends or partners about their experiences and feelings. They take new learnings home to their children and report back to me on the children's successes in later sessions. Yes, we women like to talk – it's official!

Men (and women): Don't fight the monkeys

Guys, if you've made previous attempts to rid yourself of @(O_O)@ they may have involved fighting as hard as possible to try and beat them. You try to ignore them or overcome by tackling them head on.

The problem with this approach is firstly that it doesn't always work, and secondly that it's very tiring, especially if you're frequently in front of an audience. For example, as a trainer and mentor, if I found it tiring I couldn't possibly do my job. Public speaking doesn't have to be tiring or hard work (That doesn't mean you don't have to prepare!). So, if you want to change and tame the @(O_O)@, then get them on your side, befriend them and speaking will become less strenuous – in fact you may find that you start to enjoy it.

Monkey taming is not a case of winning or losing; it's a "win-win" negotiation technique.

I'm making light of the male and female responses here but, to be fair, we probably exhibit a mix of behaviours depending on the situation, where we are and how safe we feel. Either way, take the learning and use whatever you need to take you to the next step on the speaking journey.

We all know that speaking in public makes many people anxious or nervous partly because it's often seen as "something new". People haven't done it before; they haven't spoken in that situation before or to that many people or on that specific topic. Speaking isn't something that's the same each time because it will by its very nature be a different experience for you and the audience each time. That's OK but you need to know how to cope with that and adapt each time in order to be successful. It's natural to have some feelings of apprehension when doing something new and most people label those feelings "nerves".

I prefer to speak about the feeling of hormones running around your body, because "nerves" are often viewed as a negative thing inside our minds. I don't believe the answer is to feel nothing inside before presenting – rather to be more aware of the feelings (or hormones) running through our bodies. We don't need to judge them as good or bad, just recognise their presence and use them to help in the situation.

Generally when I work with clients we begin to see that "being nervous" is not a helpful behaviour but that it *is* helpful to understand and recognise those feelings.

> **Monkey taming is not a case of winning or losing; it's a "win-win" negotiation technique.**

Fear is fast and infectious

Humans only have to experience something once to instantly develop a fear (that's how a phobia starts – from one incident). Let's go back for a moment to the times of cave dwelling: if lions were a threat to our children then it might be wise to be fearful of them and avoid them where possible. Maybe we'd tell our children to run away quickly or hide if they saw one. You can see how learning quickly is of benefit in this example, right? We want to protect our children from harm so if we learnt slowly we might run out of children before we learn all the lessons!

It may be that it wasn't actually a presentation that made you scared – it could have been anything from a school play to reading aloud in class: any incident that made you feel less than comfortable in front of other people.

Also we don't even have to experience the fear ourselves. We can "catch" it from other people who have fears! Learning from others' experience is great because if someone else in my village is injured by a lion I can learn how dangerous they are without having to experience it myself – *phew!* But in some instances learning from others isn't so great; even if you haven't done much public speaking, you may have "learnt" to develop a fear by noticing the people around you or your family voicing their own fears.

Astute parents reading this book will probably be wondering how to avoid passing on their fear of public speaking to their children. Well the first immediate step you can take is to make sure you don't feed the monkeys. The second, most positive, step is to continue to learn this technique and then, once you've mastered it, you can help your children do so too.

Everyone has adrenaline

Most people, at any level of seniority, are a little apprehensive before speaking. Some have been doing it so long that they're now well used to it, but ask them about their first or early experiences and there are very few stories that don't involve a large amount of fear, nerves or apprehension. My personal view is that if you don't have a little bit of adrenaline you aren't pushing yourself hard enough to grow and develop. And that's one of the reasons why I started to get involved in stand up comedy – to push my boundaries.

Because I've worked in communications for many years, I've seen hundreds of people just as they're about to go on stage; I've seen senior executives who are as nervous as anyone else. I've seen people launch new products at sales conferences who really know their stuff inside out but are still shaking with fear. I've heard them months before a big conference, staging and setting up the events or on the fly as they have to give impromptu talks. And I've spoken to them afterwards in "wash-up" meetings (I must look up where that phrase came from!). I've spent time with mentoring clients, understanding the depth of their fears, and seen all of them overcome them anyway. The point I'm making is that it's more common than you think, and unless you've got a job like mine where people share their fears, you're unlikely to know just how many people suffer from it.

Start to think of those people around you. The ones you might look at and say, "It's alright for them... They aren't nervous at all; they look really confident". Let me tell you that they might be even more nervous than you! Yes, just because they *appear* confident and loud that doesn't mean they are. In fact those of you who know me personally are aware that I'm quite a "loud" character and, while you might not believe me, I've actually quietened down since I became more confident! The type of confidence I mean is that inner confidence; that feeling inside of being OK with who you are and how well (or not so well) you do on each occasion.

Whatever level of fear or nerves you suffer from, it's important to know that it's OK that you've experienced some of these feelings. Many of the world's most famous presenters and actors say they suffer from stage fright. Most people, even experienced presenters, have some "adrenaline" when presenting in front of a group. It has been said that Michael Douglas, as he was beginning his acting career, would throw up before every performance and apparently Barbara Streisand forgot some lyrics to several of her songs during a 1967 performance and didn't do any more live performances for over 25 years. BUT IT DOESN'T NEED TO BE LIKE THIS.

There are only two fears we're born with: Falling (not heights, just falling) and loud noises. So that means that any others are either fears we have generated ourselves, inside our heads or they're down to excessive adrenaline. Luckily this means that if there are any fears we want to get rid of we can do that too. It certainly isn't natural to experience excessive fear in situations where it isn't appropriate – such as speaking!

You don't need the fear

> ## The fear is not helping you or protecting you –
> ## in fact it's preventing you from doing what you need or
> ## want to do.

The fear is not helping you or protecting you – in fact it's preventing you from doing what you need or want to do. Some people think the fear's essential for protection, but actually it "inter-fears" with the flight and fight mechanism because it can make you freeze and it exaggerates the need to talk about it so that soon no one will want to hear you. What we want to achieve by the end of this programme is an appropriate amount of adrenaline for the task in hand – you might call it "harnessing your fear and reining it in".

Some people think fear is only one way to motivate yourself and, yes, for many it can be a good thing – if you use it to give you the push to perform better. Fear can make people prepare, ensure they take the appropriate amount of care and due diligence in preparing and practising the talk. The problem comes when the level of fear is totally disproportionate to the task in hand. I'd suggest you want to approach presentations in the future with the appropriate amount of adrenaline or cortisol – just the right amount, that is in proportion and which gives you enough motivation to prepare, practise and do everything in your power to make it go well.

The other way to motivate yourself is by harnessing your fear (or adrenaline) to head *towards* your goals (instead of <u>moving away from</u> fear). That's why we look next at what you want to achieve and why there's another section on the future at the end of this book covering your new goals following your "monkey taming". If you use fear a lot at the moment to motivate yourself, start to build a picture in your mind of all the positive things that could start to happen once you overcome your fear of speaking.

The difference with strong presenters isn't that they don't have some mini monkeys sometimes, just that have fewer of them and they use the tools and techniques I'm sharing to overcome them more quickly and easily than others. Adrenaline still pays people a visit when they are trying new or different things, but simply knowing you can overcome its effects is very empowering; knowing that once you put your mind to it you can overcome the fear and manage it. That means you can stay on the positive upward spiral more easily and continue to see more and more success.

Why this programme will work for you

Well over 97% of the people who've used this process feel significantly more confident about presenting and speaking than they did before and go on to deliver calm and confident presentations or talks. After learning this, you'll have an easy technique you can always use to get rid of any fears and nerves. I'm not saying they'll disappear the first time forever, but the same ones should not reappear in the same situations. It's possible that new ones might appear when we try new things, and that's perfectly normal – we might be apprehensive, for example, because of the hormones running around our bodies. The difference is that this programme will give you the techniques and the process by which you tame the monkeys. Whenever they arise. Every time. Forever.

Many people I speak to find that before they learn this technique the only way they could speak in public was to cover up their fears and press on regardless. If that's you, then you obviously have guts and determination – so this programme will work really well. The main thing I want you to add to that determination is a proven technique. So instead of using your energy to just plough through a talk, use it to get you through this programme. The problem with covering up your fears is that your brain's bursting at the seams thinking about the fear and @(O_O)@ so it that it's hard to think about the audience and what they want. Thinking ahead to potential challenges and overcoming any unforeseen circumstances becomes almost impossible because there's no headspace left. By Taming the Monkeys your mind becomes free to think of a million and one other things that will make you a much better communicator, able to handle anything thrown your way.

Some people I speak to worry that they're so much worse at speaking than anyone else. My belief is that there really aren't many bad speakers – only effective and less effective speaking behaviours. It is not the speaker personally who's "rubbish"; it's the means and way in which they're choosing to communicate that isn't working yet. They may be articulate people who just haven't learnt to speak well in front of others or who have had poor examples to learn from. Perhaps they didn't know their reason for speaking so they didn't place any importance on communicating effectively. This process will take you through every step you need in order to become good and confident at speaking in front of others.

I have worked with many hundreds of people in group situations as well as one to one, and the secrets I share in this book are an anthology of those techniques. By following the process, you'll learn many truly effective ways to train your monkeys to behave much better. The temptation is now perhaps to just jump straight in at Chapter 5 where we start the actual process of Taming the Monkeys, but these initial chapters are just as important to lay the right foundations for success.

You might be tempted to go direct to Chapters 6, 7 & 8, where I share lots of tips and techniques but I believe these guidelines have maximum impact only AFTER the monkeys have been tamed. Otherwise the messages are largely rejected by our minds, no matter how good the tips are. For example, if a client "believes" that they aren't any good at public speaking then no matter what tools or skills they've just learnt they won't be confident enough to use them when they next speak. They will revert to the safest and easiest approach for them as always – reading from notes or PowerPoint® slides with little thought for what the audience wants.

Before you start taming you need to know a little more about the @(O_O)@ , which we'll look at now, and then to understand what's the best mindset for success (Covered in Chapter 3).

Innovative practices – Public Speaking Monkeys®

Taming your personal @(O_O)@ is the critical first level so you can get rid of the fear. It's absolutely essential that this step comes first. To be the best speaker you can be you'll want to have tamed your @(O_O)@ first before you adopt any further skills. Once they've been tamed we can start to train the monkeys, sharing techniques that work.

My concept of the Public Speaking Monkeys enables you to overcome your fears using a light-hearted, effective and memorable approach. No burying of @(O_O)@ is allowed: instead they must be tamed! Catch them, connect with them and challenge them so that their hold on you melts away.

- **Light-hearted** – In traditional presentation skills training the fear of public speaking stops many people even thinking about signing up to improve their skills and overcome those fears. They feel nervous and scared, apprehensive about what they might be asked to do on a course and some even tell me they used to feel a little embarrassed and silly that they had those fears. I decided that perhaps a more light-hearted approach than traditional courses would encourage people to address their issues or at least become curious to learn a little more. I decided to adopt an idea I'd used previously when teaching a family to speak without fear. After all, perhaps you, like me, are just a big kid on the inside!

- **Easy to grasp** – I helped the family to articulate their innermost fears of public speaking by representing the fear through another "voice". This monkey approach gets to the unconscious mind in an entertaining way, explaining how @(O_O)@ represent negative internal voices that put doubt into your mind about your public speaking abilities. I knew it would work with adults too after I first tested out the idea in an open course and Katrina, one of the participants, commented, "Public Speaking Monkeys? I've got a whole JUNGLE FULL OF THEM!"

- **Effective** – @(O_O)@ are also useful in breaking down specific beliefs people have, like the idea that mistakes and failure are bad and that people will laugh at you if you make a mistake. I use the monkey approach to help to chip away at the conditioning that leads people to experience fear whenever they think about speaking or standing up to present. Because the monkeys speed up the understanding of what causes each individual's fear, significantly more can be achieved in a far shorter time with long lasting benefits.

- **Memorable** – because you can see the @(O_O)@ and hear their voices, the whole concept becomes much more memorable. In order to be effective long term you need to learn and practise this technique as you go through the book. However, as you continue to push yourself to achieve more you might need to use these monkey management techniques in the future. Whenever you do something new it's perfectly natural to have "a bit of the monkeys" but with these very same techniques that you're learning now, you'll have the skill and ability to tame any monkey that might swing your way in the future.

Traditional approaches

There are thousands of wise words and rules written about public speaking, and having studied many of the top authors I tend to like most of their ideas and concepts. Some of the main approaches are to encourage the speaker to be mindful of their audience and not bore them to death with a 150-slide-long PowerPoint® presentation, which I think is fair to say is a commonly shared wish from audiences worldwide.

When it comes to strict rules on font size or anything similar, my general approach would be to do what works. Try different approaches and see how the audience reacts. See if it suits your style, then use it.

Towards the end of the book I've shared plenty of beneficial techniques that will make a significant difference to anyone beginning the journey to improved speaking: the most popular approaches; the ones participants have said were well-worthwhile learning and which many are still using today.

If you have a fear of public speaking then perhaps you've already read a few books on the subject, but that hasn't made you any less nervous, has it? Perhaps you've been on a course where you had to stand up and speak in front of others? Sometimes, if it's not done in the right way, that can even make the fear worse. In fact, one delegate showed up at one of my in-house presentations skills courses with a fear of presentations skills courses!

Often books tell you to relax before speaking, but don't tell you HOW. This programme tells you step by step HOW to lose your fears and nerves around speaking.

I believe *the challenge of overcoming the fear inside your head must be the FIRST THING to be addressed before adding new skills or other learnings and techniques.* People tell me this isn't addressed in other books and if it is they tell you WHAT to do but don't show you HOW. I want to share with you why it's important, what you need to do and how you can go ahead and do it, while answering any questions that might pop up along the way.

I do also believe that no piece of information or learning is used best in isolation. Often if there's a challenge or problem to be overcome it's good to consider taking the best bits from different areas and making a "new and improved" version for whatever you want to overcome. Use all of your past learning and knowledge alongside this model if you choose.

> ### *If I have seen further, it is by standing on the shoulders of giants.*
>
> Isaac Newton (1642 – 1727)

However, beware if you see conflicting information – don't be tempted not to take in this new information just because it's not been seen before. Give the techniques in this book a go and see if they work. Then use the techniques that work and only then do you need to drop any old beliefs that no longer work for you.

It's all in the mind

I hate to tell you this but the solutions to your problems are unlikely to be purely "logical". So those of you who like Mister Spock-type logic might have to let that go for a little while. Sorry! Some of my clients, such as accountants and academics, are naturally extremely logical thinkers, so sometimes they take a little longer to let go of the logic and go with the flow. They always do let go though. Eventually!

The thing is, if there were a purely logical solution to the problem you face, you'd have already resolved it yourself by now, wouldn't you?

There *is* a lot of logic involved though and before we get into the "go with the flow" approach to taming your monkeys, I think it's important that we learn a little more about how our minds create these nerves and fears and hence how the @(O_O)@ are structured. That way when we come to tame the @(O_O)@ we get a deeper understanding of the process.

Because the problem was created in our minds, it is also the place where the solution has to come from. This Taming the Monkeys process combines proven knowledge of how the mind works in order to guide you in resolving your own monkey issues. I have blended NLP* techniques used by professionals around the world with both traditional and innovative practices to make learning as fun, fast and effective as possible.

NLP (Neuro Linguistic Programming)

Most people either haven't heard of NLP or aren't quite sure what it is, so if you haven't heard of it that's OK – you are "most people!" Partly its low awareness might be down to the unattractive name. But don't let that get in the way of seeing the real benefits it can bring to improving communications with ourselves and those around us. As a Master Practitioner and Trainer of NLP with years of experience I'm passionate about the subject. I'm also honoured to be the Marketing Director for the Association for NLP, a Community Interest Company keen to promote ethics, integrity, professionalism and standards within the world of NLP.

If you're curious and want to know more about NLP, I'd highly recommend you visit www.ANLP.org where there are definitions, case studies, recommended reading and so much more. I could write the rest of the book on the virtues of NLP but plenty of other brilliant authors have done so already! In the meantime, for the purposes of this book, NLP uses knowledge of unconscious thought (the kind of thoughts we may not be so aware of) to influence the way we think and behave, thus the results we get.

The fear of public speaking and nervousness created around it is firstly all about how we THINK about speaking; the pictures and stories (or nightmares) that we play out in our minds and tell ourselves over and over again.

NLP provides the tools to identify and then deconstruct these stories so that we can start to "programme" ourselves with more useful (and realistic) stories and beliefs. You don't need to know any more other than to feel secure in the knowledge that I'm bringing the benefits of NLP to you in easy steps through the Taming the Monkeys process.

For more information on NLP training email me direct - Dee@DeeClayton.com

---

"Monkey Tail"

Leonora Stokes - Managing Director at Roar Accounting Ltd

"As a business owner of 10 years standing, it has always been important for me to present well to clients, but recently I have wanted to take the business to new levels, to grow and expand and gain new clients. I knew that presenting at conferences and events was vital to my business growth strategy but there was a problem - I was terrified of speaking in public. Even the thought of speaking made me suffer <u>terrible physical effects. I felt nervous, sick and panicky even to the point where fainting was not uncommon.</u> *To make it worse I needed to talk about accountancy topics like money laundering and tax advice - not always seen as the most stimulating topics!*

I saw Dee speak at an event where she explained about the "Public Speaking Monkeys". She also talked about the importance of sharing our business message in a personal and unique way. Her message was very relevant to me and her approach seemed light-hearted yet effective...By the end of the sessions I had practised several speeches and felt confident and calm about speaking in public. I had a structure and approach I knew worked every time. A few months ago I spoke at a huge conference and it was great. I got my point over articulately and as a result I gained several new leads and I'm now planning more talks for the coming months. I highly recommend Dee and her approach to taming those pesky monkeys!"

The 3 steps to speaking excellence

My approach to speaking excellence is split into three levels to help people first lose their presentation fear and then become a skilled and strong speaker. This book focuses on the first of the three levels: Taming and training your monkeys, losing your fears and gaining confidence. Also, I share people's stories throughout the book so you can apply those learnings to your own situations too.

Step 1: Taming and training your personal Public Speaking Monkeys®

Taming your personal @(O_O)@ is the critical first level so you can get rid of the fear. After this step has been completed through finishing this book, one to one or group training sessions people have achieved their goal of being a fear-free public speaker and they go forward to become good speakers. Others, when they lose their fear, realise that they have a message they need to share. They decide to set themselves some big goals around being an excellent, effective and an enjoyable speaker to listen to.

This may seem a little far off for some of you right now (Because the @(O_O)@ are causing too much interference), but for those already interested in the long game let me just share quickly the next two steps, should you choose to take them. The next two steps to speaking excellence are:

Step 2 – Public Speaking Training Sessions for You and Your Monkey

This focuses mostly on practical changes in the way you approach presenting and helping you to practise the tricks of the trade and proven techniques in a safe environment with constructive and friendly feedback. The sessions are most often conducted face to face or through teleseminars and the wonders of video conferencing. Sessions can be in groups or on a one to one basis. **Please visit www.DeeClayton.com "courses" page for more information.**

Step 3 – Profitable Public Speaking and Monkey Mastery

Designed for business leaders and those in highly visible situations, *Mastery* enables you to get to the top of your game. It's not for everyone and only a few people are committed and focused enough to take this step. If this is of interest to you please contact me personally through the contact details in this book referencing "Mastery".

Evolution – Time to change

If anything I've mentioned so far has struck a chord with you or you've seen yourself in some of these scenarios then now really is the time to change and learn how to get rid of your fears when speaking. In this day and age, gadgets are getting more and more interesting, exciting and dynamic. To be heard above the background din you must not only get over your nerves and fears but also learn how to gain and maintain attention. Like it or not, you need to change with the times.

Anyway enough of my little soapbox – I'll hop back onto it later perhaps. All you need to know for now is that anything you're experiencing is perfectly normal; other people suffer from it too and you're not alone. However, what has been the past does not have to be your future. The good news is that you can change it. You can improve – and by following this programme you *will* improve. How much is up to you.

As I mentioned earlier, over 97% of people who've completed this programme have exceeded the targets they thought possible at the beginning of the programme. So now you know where the journey's going, let's talk a little about this unique process of taming the @(O_O)@. It's all very well saying it will work but some of the more cynical people out there might tell you "Of course she's going to say that! She wants you to buy the book!"

Yes, I'm happy that you've bought the book, but only because I'm delighted that you've now started on your journey to overcoming these paralyzing fears and distracting nerves.

This book is all about helping you to filter out those voices in your head that just sound like interference. It might sound abstract. But it isn't. Through the processes in this book you can get your @(O_O)@ working on your side and even turn them into voices of reason. Training your mind to deal rationally with fear is part of a complete solution, not just a one trick wonder.

> **...get your @(O_O)@ working on your side and even turn them into voices of reason. Training your mind to deal rationally with fear is part of a complete solution, not just a one trick wonder.**

The difference with my system is we attack all sides of the problem: The Taming the Monkeys process takes you step by step through examples and exercises enabling you to successfully complete the whole change process. Once you've learnt the process you'll know how to deal with any future monkeys that may arise so you know you can do anything – you just have to repeat this technique and, as with anything, the more you do it the easier it becomes.

If you didn't want to achieve something new or do something different you wouldn't need to be reading this. By accepting that you need to improve your speaking skills, you've already made it obvious that you want to achieve something more, better or greater than you have done. Perhaps you want to break that fear of speaking or perhaps you have an important message that you want to share with others but fear is stopping you. Let's continue to see how we move from downward to upward spirals and use our own minds most effectively to overcome the fear in the next chapters.

Warning

- Don't fight the monkeys – tame them!

- Don't feed your monkeys – tame them!

- Don't feed other people's monkeys – tell them to tame them!

- Don't pass on your monkeys – tame them!

- Don't catch monkeys from others – tell them to tame them!

Key takeaways

✓ Public speaking monkeys cause physical and behavioural symptoms – you can change this

✓ Men and women react differently to stress. Recognising this helps

✓ Unreasonable or inappropriate fear and nerves are not helpful. They interrupt the natural process. Nerves and fear are natural and good when appropriate to the situation

✓ Think of "feeling nervous" as an adrenaline rush (we'll do more on that later)

✓ Good speakers become familiar with speaking, deal with monkey voices and manage the adrenaline rush

✓ The multi-award-winning concept of the Public Speaking Monkeys® is different to other approaches because the monkeys are in your mind and therefore so is the solution

✓ Using light-hearted, effective and memorable approaches you'll learn how to tame the monkeys

Chapter 3 –
Changing your mind for long term success

In this chapter we go into a little more detail about changing your mindset because now we know that the monkeys are in our minds, and if we don't like their current behaviour we'll need to change it, and thus change our minds. We know what we don't want – those negative monkey voices. So now we also need to know what's the most helpful mindset to have to tame the monkeys – if we aren't any longer going to have those negative doubts, what is the most helpful way we can use our minds to achieve success instead?

We like to think we know how to change our mind but often we aren't clear on how to do it long term. Have you ever made a New Year's resolution? Have you perhaps stuck to it for an hour, day or month, but eventually you've just gone back to how you used to be? This book helps you to lose your fear and change your attitude towards speaking **forever**. And in order to make permanent changes you need to know the secret ingredients for positive permanent change.

Below I have summarised the key ingredients we need to consider.

The recipe for learning – key ingredients

There are a few key ingredients you need to become more aware of in order to tame your monkeys easily

- **Motivation** – the energy to want to learn the new thing

- **Belief**– that you can learn it so you begin the learning process

- **Skills** – you need to know how to learn the new thing

- **Action** – a change of behaviour to begin and practice new skills

- **Feedback** – doing the new thing for real and then getting feedback

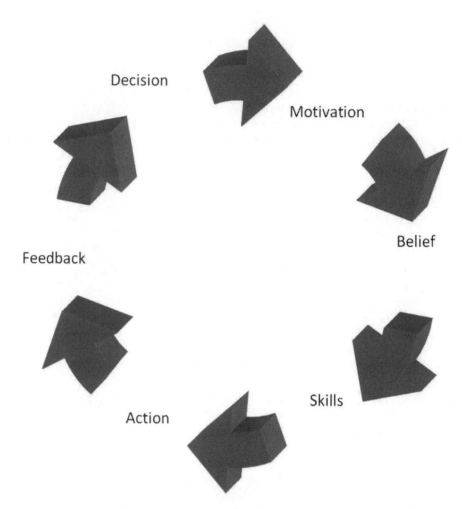

Let's look at this in more depth in the context of taming your @(O_O)@, though the diagram above is just as valid for learning the new techniques and approaches in Chapters 6, 7 & 8 – and anything else you choose to learn for that matter!

Motivation

This is the secret ingredient, the yeast that makes the bread rise. Have you ever made bread but forgot to add the yeast? It looks OK, you think everything's good to go... but in the morning you look to find just a big blob of gunk. Motivation is like yeast in bread because without it nothing will happen. If there's a project that you've been meaning to do but "haven't quite got round to it yet" then if you look deeply enough and are totally honest with yourself you may well find that you don't actually want to do it. If you haven't got the motivation, it's not going to happen.

I'm going to assume you have some motivation to tame your @(O_O)@ or you wouldn't be doing this programme, but I have no doubt that the amount of success you'll see will be directly related to how motivated you are to achieve your outcomes you identified earlier. You have to want to get rid of your nerves and fears and get rid of those negative feelings associated with speaking. Who knows, you might even want to become a really good speaker and communicator.

At this point in the game it's enough to say that we've all seen people who are and who aren't motivated to learn, haven't we? Some people aren't motivated for themselves – they've been told to do this, read that or try the other. Needless to say it never works until they're ready to learn and are motivated for their own reasons – not anyone else's. Often people have motivation at the beginning of a process, but not enough to carry them through to completion, and that's because motivation comes from having motives or things that are important to you. If what you want isn't motivating enough (i.e. a deep connection) or exciting enough, then if you hit a little obstacle along the way you might give up. When you have really motivating goals to get to on your journey, the power of the goal helps pull you through if you hit a little bump – so you find a solution and move to the next leg of the journey.

Exercise – motivation

If you want to turbo boost your motivation, write in your workbook a list of answers to the following question:

Q: What's important to me about taming the monkeys?

Continue to ask yourself this over and over until you've captured all your reasons, which should look like a list of motivations. If you like, pick the three most important ones to keep you motivated throughout this book. The answers might well be similar to your answers to earlier questions but something additional may have popped up too.

Now let's assume you have the motivation; you know why you're doing this. Once you've set in your mind what you want you will have the motivation to carry on past any bump you happen to hit on the journey. Next you need to believe you can do it; believe you can tame your monkeys easily or that you can be a confident speaker.

Belief

Beliefs are things we think are true but which in fact may not be true. For example, we may know that we aren't really "rubbish at speaking" but sometimes a part of us still keeps telling us we are. Perhaps you believe you

> ## ... a positive belief is more likely to deliver the outcome you want....

don't deserve that good job and any minute now you're going to get caught out or exposed as an impostor!

Beliefs can be helpful or they can be not so helpful. If I believe I'm going to be good at learning something new that's a more helpful belief than thinking I'm going to be bad at it. The thing is, if you're like me you may have been taught an unhelpful approach to learning or trying new things, such as, "Prepare for the worst and anything else will be a bonus" or "Under-promise and over deliver". Since my in-depth studies of NLP and having worked with so many clients, I understand more about how the mind works. I believe a positive belief is more likely to deliver the outcome you want...as long as it's accompanied by action! Remember, you don't have to broadcast everything you believe! In some cultures, such as the UK's, it's not considered polite to go around saying how wonderful you are. It's totally OK to keep it to yourself!!!

Empowering beliefs are more helpful

If we already believe we're going to learn this new technique quickly and easily then our mind set (providing we are motivated to improve continuously) would be to seek out ways to ensure we do actually learn easily (and perhaps even more easily than we expected). For example we might spend longer on the exercises, practice thinking differently, start discussing what we've learnt with others and begin feeling good about our progress.

Positive beliefs need to be accompanied by action

Many recent self-help books talk about the power of positive thinking and I think there's a lot to be said for it. But if you speak to people who are interested in the ancient Universal Laws of Attraction they'll tell you that action is an essential ingredient to getting what you want. Seems pretty obvious right? But how many people still don't take action because of fear or some other excuse? Have you heard people talk about self-help books as "shelf help books"? That's because they stay on the shelf instead of being read and put into practice.

I bet you know people who believe they're good but really aren't. You only have to watch any of the "talent" shows on TV to see somewhat sad examples of that (Even though they do make me laugh!). These are prime examples of "over-belief". They think they're great at singing but alas they can't sing at all. I happen to believe that with the right skills and beliefs in place and a lot of practice everyone CAN sing – to some degree. They haven't taken any action, or the right action, to develop the skills to do it though.

Sliding doors

If you've seen the movie *Sliding Doors* you'll know what I mean. The movie had the characters take two tiny different actions in their life and then played out the consequences of each. In the context of public speaking I want you to hold the idea that everything that's happening now in your experience of speaking – both good and bad – is happening because of an earlier action. Now, it doesn't mean that your earlier action was taken consciously or on purpose, but it was taken. For example, if when you were at school you read something out in class but made a mistake, all the other kids may have laughed at you or the teacher may have told you off. While you might think it was so long ago it doesn't matter, a "re-action" will have arisen from that event. We've all taken an action unconsciously that we thought was in our best interests (but of course we were young and had no idea whether it was good for the long term or not!). Here are some unconscious decisions we might have taken as a result of those actions without realising:

- *I'm never speaking out loud in class again*

- *I'm going to improve my reading and prove them wrong*

- *I'm going to get angry and fight back at those laughing at me*

The list of decisions is endless but we will have made one of those choices of actions, and unless we've done anything to address that decision it will still be there in our minds.

If it was a good and helpful decision, like I'm going to improve my reading, then keep it! The problem comes when the decision limits us in our ability to achieve now – these can be referred to as limiting decisions. So if the decision was never to stand up in class again then that's limiting you now in your ability to achieve your outcomes.

Following on from a limiting decision you might have created a more generalised limiting belief. For example, that incident might lead to any number of limiting beliefs such as:

- *I can't read*

- *I'm stupid*

- *I'm thick*

- *I'm no good at speaking aloud*

- *I hate people staring at me*

"Monkey Tail"

I attended a workshop a few years ago to learn even more about body language and voice. When we got there, Alistair, our trainer, told us that to best discover our speaking voices we would be singing. Not only that, but by the end of the day we'd have written our own song and performed it to the group! Well you can imagine the monkeys that popped up in my head at that point!

"You can't do it"

"You're not good enough"

"You can't sing"

"You don't know how to write a song"

"You're gonna look stupid?"

Can you see how they're all monkeys? Some are based on beliefs: I don't believe I can do it, I don't believe I can sing, etc. I noticed they weren't very helpful beliefs that my monkeys were throwing at me! I decided a better belief to tell my monkey was to just "go with the flow"; to believe that the trainer knew what he was talking about and would help us to get there... That he knew a process by which he could help me to sing even if I wasn't too sure about it yet. I chose to believe that if I followed what he said I'd be able to write and perform my own song. We'll cover the techniques on how to tame your monkeys in Chapter 4, but for now it's important to see how these monkeys create their mutterings and the impact those few words have on our beliefs and ability to access our skills!

> ## Much of this programme is about destroying those less helpful beliefs and building more helpful ones.

As you're probably beginning to see, if these aren't dealt with they become negative @(O_O)@. In short, an unhelpful decision can turn into an unhelpful general belief about yourself and so in order to eliminate it we'll want to identify it (notice it is there), acknowledge it (pay attention to what caused it) and then remove it through the Taming the Monkeys process.

"Every action has its pleasures and its price."

Socrates

Disempowering beliefs are less helpful

Imagine for a moment what it would be like if you believed everything was against you – if you didn't believe you could learn easily, you didn't believe you could find the time or even know you could do it. When you start thinking with this mindset everything feels a lot less easy doesn't it?

Then the spirals come into play again because our minds are very clever and get good at "filtering out" stuff that doesn't quite match up to our beliefs. If someone said you were good at presenting, yet you didn't believe it to be true, you might hear the comment but not allow it to sink into your mind. That's because it didn't match your beliefs. In fact you might not even *hear* it, let alone process it! Much of this programme is about destroying those less helpful beliefs and building more helpful ones.

Total responsibility

Sometimes when I begin to talk to clients about beliefs that hold you back they want to "blame" it on someone else – and perhaps that's a fairly natural first reaction. What I'm interested in is what is a "helpful" reaction? Will it help you to overcome your monkeys? In the earlier example of reading out loud, if we knew that the teacher had shouted at you for getting it wrong is it helpful to blame him or her? Often the answer is no. Is it helpful to identify the cause? Yes! And that is an important step. However, it isn't helpful to "blame" Mr Smith the teacher. There are two reasons why this blame isn't helpful:

1) It prevents you moving forward

Holding on to blame from the past is not a healthy approach – it sometimes keeps us stuck in the past instead of living in the now.

2) It reduces your power to change things

If you put the blame onto someone else you're giving them the power over the situation. If it was their fault, then by default "they" are the only ones that can change it. If however, we take responsibility for the outcome, we also take the power back to change it. So in the example we must take responsibility for deciding to take the action e.g. deciding to avoid speaking in public again. Then we have all of the power to change that decision we made and right the wrong of the past. Other than knowing what sparked it off, Mr Smith has nothing more to do with it. Forgive him!

The other thing is that Mr Smith was probably only doing his best at the time with the skills he had available. If that's how he learnt to teach, or was taught, or if it worked for other children then he was only trying to do what he thought was right at the time, even though it may well not have been the best approach. Remember none of us is perfect!

You'll notice that I've taken my time to talk to you about your motivations and beliefs because they're so critical to your success. I could have started this book at Chapter 4, where I talk about taming your monkeys but I know how important it is to ensure you have your mindset right first. You'll find it easier and faster if you go into the Taming the Monkeys process with the belief that you can do it and with an open mind. If you believe you can't overcome your fears this process will be much less easy to master.

Once you have the motivation and belief, you can always find the skills somewhere - "Assuming" whatever you want to achieve has already been achieved by man (or woman!), it's always possible to discover the skills you need. Of course many of us don't even need to be top of the field; just excellent is pretty good.

Skills

Once you have the motivation to learn and believe that you can tame your @(O_O)@, next you need to develop the skills so that you actually know how to do it. When it comes to public speaking generally, the "skills" you need can be broadly classed into one of two areas:

Skill 1 – the power of your mind

Understanding how your mind works is something that's not often talked about unless you've studied psychology or you start to follow a personal development journey where you begin to discover how our minds work.

NLP (Neuro Linguistic programming) covers many areas including that of studying how our minds work and how to use them more effectively. Many of the learnings of NLP come from something called "modelling". This process is where you study "models of excellence" or people who excel in their field. Through studying them over time you identify what elements make them truly successful. Deep modelling projects can be long processes but the end results deliver strategies and approaches that, if you adopt them, enable you to do that thing to a high standard too. You could say it delivers the rules for success.

The difference with modelling using NLP versus some other more traditional "studies" is that the workings of the person's mind are also modelled. Looking back to our circular diagram, we don't just look at skills i.e. how a great speaker might craft his words, how many words he uses in a sentence or how quickly he speaks. If you look on the Internet there are countless reviews and analyses of Barack Obama's speeches – and it's a very helpful and logical approach to evaluating speeches. However it's not the only approach and shouldn't be used in isolation.

We also want to model the **motivation and beliefs** that are deep within the person so we can uncover what's driving those skills. That's what NLP enables people to do to: identify which motivations and beliefs are helpful. That means when I share with you, for example, the notion that positive beliefs are more helpful, it isn't just from my own experience. It's "wisdom" from NLP studies that have modelled thousands of successful people in all sorts of different fields from politics to sport and business to healthcare.

When you optimise how you use your mind you will really start to power up your messages, your communication and your personality on stage. This technique you're learning allows you to start to identify what motivations and beliefs are inside *your* mind that help you or are preventing you from becoming successful.

Use the power of imagination

For many of the exercises we're going to want to use our imagination – and using it is a skill that's more developed in some than others. When we were young I believe we all had an active imagination – and then something happened called "growing up" and all of a sudden, and depending on your choices, your imagination may have expanded or been tucked away in a box under the bed! For this process to work it's important to add a little imagination into the mix. I know that might sound a little odd, but bear with me here...

Imagine you've been asked to give an important presentation at short notice. You might think about it, worry about it and imagine a million and one ways in which it can go wrong. Then perhaps you try to ignore it, hope it will go away and put it out of your mind.

But does it really leave your mind or does it just lurk about at the back somewhere? By taking the "leave it" approach you may have made things even worse. After all, there's been no planning, no practising and certainly no consideration of what the audience wants. You haven't spared a thought for what hand-outs need producing, let alone how to make the talk interesting and engaging.

 A little while before the presentation, perhaps the night before or shortly before you have to talk, you might begin to recognise that it is in fact true; you really are going to have to present (Though the alternative of running out the fire escape at the side of the room is looking pretty attractive!).

All of a sudden it's becoming reality... Perhaps your @(O_O)@ start to go into one..."You should have prepared!", "You can't do this!", "You'll run out of things to say!", "They only want a 20-minute speech but that's ages – best to just reel off everything you know about the topic in no apparent order!" and so on and so on...

Of course, because there was no preparation, the presentation might not go that well. Perhaps it runs over time – you don't know where you are in your presentation. Maybe you've got flustered and then read from your notes. All in all you know you've let yourself down. You could have done better. In fact you hate presenting and vow to never do it again. Then you get even more worried the next time you have to do a presentation because you remember how bad it was last time. It can only be worse this time because it's even more important to even more people – *I hate public speaking.* Sound familiar?

The whole presentation's gone horribly wrong and you haven't even started it yet. Your imagination has run wild. You don't know for sure that all these bad things really are going to happen do you? But it still feels real doesn't it?

Even though you know some of it's irrational you still get real feelings of fear, anxiety and nervousness, don't you? So how powerful is the imagination? Even as you heard the story above perhaps you started to get those feelings, or could really empathize with that story. So you can see how powerful the imagination is now. And if just imagining it brings on those disempowering feelings, surely we can work with the imagination to *take away* those feelings too. Of course, the feelings are there for a reason and this will all become clear when we begin to tame our @(O_O)@.

"Monkey Tail"

The end of the day was fast approaching and we all knew that soon it would be the time when we had to stand up and sing in front of the group. We'd learnt the skills, uncovered a motivation, got ourselves some more helpful beliefs and we were ready. We just needed to do the behaviour of following the process and seeing if it worked. Without actually getting up there and performing my own song I'd not have known if it worked. I needed to test it out in the "real world".

OK, so it was a training room, but for me it was the real world. Real people watching me and waiting for me to sing them my song. I offered to go first to get it over and done with. It didn't go well. I felt awkward, embarrassed, fearful and silly! Alistair said, "Well done for getting up there and going first but what happened to everything I just taught you today?" Without realising, in a moment of stress, I'd just gone back to the old way of doing things. In this case singing in my old way and hoping I'd get a different result. Well it doesn't take a genius to know that won't work!

His advice then followed: "Dee just do the process we learnt, believe in it and see what happens. Change your body language – how would you be standing if you knew you could do it"? This time I was amazed at what came out of my mouth. Don't get me wrong, I won't be signing up for talent shows anytime soon, but I was in tune and it felt great!!! As we progressed through the rest of the group we all learnt the same thing: do it the old way and it doesn't work. Follow the new process, believe you can do it and it works!

The following week at a networking group there was a competition for the best 1 minute business introduction. Now I know you won't feel much empathy for me, but the "You're a presentation skills trainer you better give a great pitch" monkey paid me a visit. Instead of my usual approach I sang my one-minute song with new words to the tune of Twelve Days of Christmas! I needed to get over a few monkeys to do it, but I kept my pride and I won a bottle of wine for my efforts! That's taking action!

Skill 2 – practical skills

The second kind of skills required are the more traditional practical ones. When it comes to public speaking most people have learnt by watching others. This is a wonderful way of learning if the people you're watching are very good at what they do. However when it comes to public speaking, many people are not strong. This means that not only might you have fears and nerves to overcome yourself but also you might not have had strong role models to copy.

The aim of this book, as mentioned earlier, is to tame your monkeys so that you can go ahead and take action to stand up and do your presentation without @(O_O)@ filling your head completely. If and when they do pop up you'll have all the tools and abilities to be able to converse with them and get them working for you.

I also cover practical skills in Chapters 6, 7 & 8, sharing some of the best-practice speaking tips and techniques with you to get you started on a very strong footing. I've taken them from the elements that participants on my courses have found most useful. Do they give you everything you need to know to be excellent speaker? No, that's for another book! Do Chapters 6, 7 & 8 provide you with a very strong basis to go ahead and be a very good speaker and start the process of taking action? Yes!

Action

The next ingredient in the mix is *action*. Positive thinking alone is not an effective presentation technique! The mindset that's healthiest is one that says, "I'm already good at speaking, I can speak in public and I'd like to continue to become even better".

"Monkey Tail"

Recently I was working alongside a fabulous NLP trainer and friend of mine, Bryce Redford. He trains in the area of change management and is highly trained and skilled in using the "arrow break" process to demonstrate his point (excuse the pun!). Don't try this at home but he teaches people how to safely and easily break a real archery arrow on their throat.

Before I did it I was nervous and apprehensive; I didn't really believe it was possible. But then I saw other people do it and I stepped forward with a full belief that I could do it and it snapped into two. The interesting thing about the exercise is that if you don't fully believe you can do, it the arrow just bends until you decide to do it for real and then it snaps easily into pieces.

Sometimes we avoid taking action because we don't like change. Humans naturally like to build up routines and approach things in the same or similar way. When we wake up in the morning we probably do all the same morning tasks such as dressing, brushing our teeth and making breakfast, and in the same order most of the time. This makes things easier for our minds – the routine means we don't have to think about every little detail of life all the time. But now think what it's like when you sleep over somewhere new such as in a hotel room or at someone's house. You have to think about where you put things and even in which direction the toilet is! We have to think about change to begin with, and fairly quickly it becomes more natural as we repeat the action again and again. I think it's because the first time you do something it feels a little bit different that many people don't like to do new things. In fact most people would rather do things the old way, knowing it won't work, than do it the new way and risk that perhaps it won't be perfect first time. That's ironic really because what they're doing now is far from perfect!

You need to take action to learn and complete this book – you need to do the exercises and then later the most important action will happen once you complete this book (or during the process of reading this book) when you stand up and deliver a presentation in front of friends or colleagues. It will be at that point that you begin to implement what you've learnt in real life and discover how well the process is working for you.

If you always do what you've always done, you'll always get what you've always got. You know that saying, right? But it's motivation and drive that will see you past this mini-hurdle. And it *is* a mini-hurdle because mostly AFTER the event it's never as bad as you thought, but before you tackle the problem it seems huge. Remember that often we only think it's a big hurdle because we haven't done it yet. That's the fear of the unknown.

Assuming you're in charge of your mind... and now you know about beliefs... even if you aren't fond of change, for example, you can start to question your beliefs and make them more helpful. Notice how open children are to trying new things and how you praise them when they try something new and learn – even if they don't get it totally right first time. Start to see everywhere in your life where doing new things and change has actually been a good thing.

Feedback

It is essential to get feedback on your actions. Just because someone's been speaking in public for 20 years that doesn't mean they're good at public speaking. It means that if they haven't received any feedback they've been practising the same thing for 20 years – good or bad.

Practice doesn't make perfect – practice makes permanent.

> ## Practice doesn't make perfect – practice makes permanent.

If you're doing something wrong – or not as well as you could be – then repeating that negative undesired behaviour for over 20 years won't help the situation. It does quite the opposite – it begins to ingrain and embed that less positive habit or behaviour. If you're not told that something could be better or that there's a better way of doing things, how are you to know you need to change?

Feedback can either be external from the audience, from your friends and colleagues, or internal – you can give yourself feedback. When giving yourself feedback it's important that you've already tamed your @(O_O)@. Up until that point your feedback's unlikely to be balanced; like many people I work with, you may be too harsh on yourself.

Next you will learn how to use the feedback sandwich (No, not the s**t sandwich as some people call it!). This sandwich gives you the ability to feedback either to yourself or others in a manner that will feel nice. It will maintain the upward spiral in yourself or the person to whom you're giving feedback.

The best place to get to is the mindset where you really love feedback; you see it as a gift from the person giving it. Now at this point I realise that some people might be saying to themselves "Yeah right!" but believe me I know how you feel. Why is it that so many of us see feedback as a bad thing, or at least not very good? Why do most of us hate the idea of getting feedback? I talk about this in my workshops – I'm always asking who likes to get feedback and mostly very few put up their hands. When I ask why not, most people say it makes them feel bad or that they don't like getting told off.

So I started to wonder why so many people feel bad about feedback (including little old me!).

To many, feedback means criticism

When I was growing up there wasn't much mention of over-complimenting children and saying how wonderful they were all of the time. Mostly at school we were praised if we did something extraordinarily well (pretty rare for me as an "average" student") and told off or criticised when things didn't go as well as the teacher had hoped.

For many of the people I speak to there isn't really a "neutral ground" for feedback. You've either done well or not well. And of course it's often easier to remember the bad bits. Feedback in my day definitely didn't seem to be standard practice. Even in the corporate world of work, you got an annual appraisal, and perhaps more often than that in some of the more forward thinking companies, but very rarely did you get feedback with the sole purpose of improving your performance – i.e. not linked to your pay review or a current problem.

The result in our minds therefore is if people only give feedback when something's wrong, the person receiving feedback can develop a connection (or an anchor as it is called in NLP) between feedback and failure or disappointment. We come to believe that people can only be bothered to give us feedback when they're disappointed with our performance. Perhaps we didn't score that goal, run fast enough or get a high enough grade. So perhaps you've learnt to associate feedback automatically with bad feedback. After all, when was the last time you had good feedback? What percentage of good to bad feedback do you think we experience? The UK culture is particularly guilty of this where it seems not to be OK to say you're doing well. Apparently, when a child is growing up they hear the word "NO" twenty times more often than they hear the word "YES". If this is the case, is it any wonder we associate feedback with not doing things correctly or in the manner others would like us to do it in?

"Monkey Tail"

Recently I've done quite a bit of work with a major Japanese car manufacturer. What I really liked was the manner in which they ensure their cars are of exceptional quality. They follow a "Kaizen" approach where they check each part of the production process and feedback to colleagues, bosses and workers alike, no matter what their rank.

They speak and communicate about levels of quality hitting the right standards – then they learn and move forward. They don't wait for the whole car to be manufactured, only to find out too late that there is a better way to do things. Instead they improve as they go along. Little by little if needs be, but always improving or measuring standards.

Now I know you aren't making a car and speaking is a little less black and white, but the message of constant improvement is still valid.

The feedback sandwich that tastes nice

"So what is the solution?" I hear you ask. Luckily there's a simple, easy solution: the feedback sandwich. It probably isn't the same as ones you've heard or read about before, though it may be similar.

The feedback sandwich goes a bit like this:

1. **An overall positive comment about a specific thing that went really well**

2. **Up to three things that would make it even better next time**

3. **Finished off with an overall positive comment about the person themselves.**

The great thing about the feedback sandwich is it works brilliantly when you give feedback to friends, children and to yourself – even if you know you're doing it. I always use this as much as possible with myself and often find myself correcting anything I might say that's less helpful. This is how you need to speak to the @(O_O)@ too. Instead of listening to their chatter, I encourage you to adapt what you hear into the feedback sandwich – but more about that later.

Feedback sandwich in everything

I've introduced NLP already, and it's interesting to know at this stage of the book some of the techniques you'll be adopting. Much of my work is based on NLP and the helpful tools, techniques and beliefs involved in that art and science of learning.

Among the things you learn about early on in NLP training are beliefs, ideas or mindsets you may want to adopt in order to see more success (Called presuppositions for the NLP-keen among you). The great thing is you don't even have to believe in these ways of working! I mean, it's not a religion, and no one will judge you whether you believe them or not. But what NLP does suggest is that if you *act as if they're true you will experience better results.* It took me a while to get my head around that one! Act as if they're true. That sounded odd to me, to carry things around in my head not knowing whether they were true or not... but you get used to it after a while!

The more I got to know about NLP the more I found that I could carry different ideas around in my head, even if many of them were contradictory. The point is to use the right thought or idea at the right time. And what *is* the right thought or idea? Well that depends, but really if it works then use it. If it gets the result you want, use it. The following belief has really changed my life and outlook, and I'm not exaggerating. I hope you benefit from it as much as I did, and still am.

"There is no failure – only feedback"

If, for a moment, you can see this as "true" in your mind's eye then consider this – you can never ever fail again, and you never have! How cool is that! You can see any response you get to anything as feedback. If things don't go so well in your talk or presentation you can just see that as feedback – perhaps you'll have to change your way of thinking about things. For example, you might now think to yourself, "I'd better do it differently next time", or "I've learnt from that so I won't do that again!"

Without my "failure-not-feedback" attitude, I don't think I'd have adapted so quickly from a corporate career to the world where I run my own business. The human mind's a wonderful thing but we need to make sure we don't use it as an excuse not to act quickly and easily. It's important to see feedback for what it is: just someone's opinion. You can be upset by negative feedback and use it to fuel the downward spiral of self-doubt. OK, that's an option, but a pretty unhelpful one if you want to move forward and be a successful speaker. The audience might say it was wonderful but maybe although you know most of it was good, you still want to change the way you did something. Well that's OK too. By gaining feedback, you can immediately change what you're doing. Remember, you only want to practice if you know you're doing the right things. Add feedback into the loop of practising so that you adapt quickly.

Almost all comedians, when they're new and starting to create sets, use a voice recorder and then listen back to performances to hear where people laughed and where there were unfortunate silences! I found it a very useful way to develop and improve my own stand-up comedy performances. The most important thing I learned was not that people weren't laughing; it was that I wasn't leaving a long enough gap to allow for their laughing before I moved on to the next line. I guess if I was getting laughs I should really milk them!

There are plenty of ways for you to get feedback, either from a buddy or on your own, especially with new technology like video and voice recorders. Record yourself and listen back to it, asking where did the audience appreciate what I did and what could be even better?

Your Response

The final piece of the puzzle is deciding how you'll respond to feedback: here are the choices you have...

1. **Do nothing –** you don't agree with the feedback anyway. This is perfectly fine. Often, the greatest people of their time were not initially understood by their peers. Experience says the thing here is to be aware of how many times you received that repeated feedback. I know of someone who's been trying to set up their business and for two years has been receiving similar feedback from all sorts of people. Things like "It's a great idea, but how will you make money from it?"The point is you need to be able to take a balanced look at the feedback. Is it too negative? Is it too positive? Are you reacting appropriately?

2. **Take it on board –** the next thing you can do with feedback is act upon it. Change something. I had to do that with my original business idea. I needed to adapt the idea to make it work for the audience. While it isn't a million miles off where I am now, I took on board what I'd learnt, which meant I tripled my year one turnover in year two and doubled it again in year three.

3. **Get upset by it –** Whatever your response, there's an impact on your motivation. So if you make a decision to improve your public speaking to learn more and take on board comments, then motivation will increase because you're getting nearer. Unfortunately not everyone delivers feedback in the form of the feedback sandwich – so it doesn't always feel so good. Sometimes we get feedback that discourages us because we take it as personal criticism. That could lead to de-motivation and throw us off-track so we don't proceed with our objectives or we become paralysed with self-doubt and slip into the downward spiral. It's at this point that your goals come in and really help you get back on track. If you've had what you perceive as negative feedback, then by visualising or reminding yourself of your goals you can regain the buoyancy and strength to get through these choppy waters.

The reaction you decide to take is a small link in the chain but it's a very important one. It's important that we're consciously aware of the decision we take and how that impacts on motivation. Learn to take feedback well and you learn to have it only increase your motivation. I'm not saying this will happen straight away; sometimes when I receive feedback my initial reaction's to beat myself up. But because I know about monkeys I make a conscious choice to make sure that I have a chat with them so that any negative feelings are short-lived. By turning the @(O_O)@ around and helping them to be on my side I ensure things start to improve. Some people naturally use their minds in this way and are totally motivated, but many people need a little bit of extra monkey focus and practice on this topic. The only true mistake you can make when becoming a stronger speaker is to give up trying! That's why feedback should be something we love, but mostly it tends to be something we don't look forward to. Let's change that attitude.

Watch your thoughts
They become words

Watch your words
They become actions

Watch your actions
They become habits

Watch your habits
They become your character

Watch your character
It becomes your destiny

~ Frank Outlaw

How to complete this programme successfully

In Chapter 4 we see the actual process of taming the monkeys, but these initial chapters are just as important to lay the right foundations for success. Just before we move to the specifics, the final thing I want to share with you are some recommendations and advice on how to complete this programme successfully. Follow the instructions!

1. Read this book from front to back and in order. If you don't read the whole book you might miss out some important stuff!

    This is a very active process – you need *to actually do it*. There's no point in reading the book and not doing the exercises. Even though I say this, it's amazing the number of people who still do that. They're the kind of people who like to observe life but not to join in. I want to encourage you right off the bat to join in. Do every exercise to the best of your ability. That doesn't mean perfectly – it means to the best of your ability.

    If you don't follow the instructions (just like baking a cake) things might not turn out how you expected. The successful people have followed the instructions and all the steps in this process and completed all the exercises properly. For example, they've written things down when told to, which makes the learnings more effective and prevents us from "cheating" ourselves. If you aren't following the instructions in this process, ask yourself why not.

2. If you've tried something similar before but it didn't work – remember, you need the right mindset to Tame the Monkeys first before you learn the new skills. Look at any "successful" person's life story, whether they're a sporting hero, a pop star, a political figure or a businessperson. Whoever it is you admire, I'm willing to take a guess that they didn't just make it big first time. We may think it looks like that because we've only just seen them, but really if you look at their life story they've probably been "at it" for years trying to find the right approach; the one that works. That's not just years of practice – because remember practice doesn't make perfect, practice makes permanent – it's years of seeking out the right teachers and then taking on feedback and adapting to reach their goals.

3. Be patient and measure your success. There are definitely different levels of fear and nerves, and I'm not expecting

you to get rid of all your monkeys immediately. Some clients see a gradual reduction as they progress through the programme. There are often some blinding flashes of revelation so look out for them too. It's a bit like a game of snakes and ladders. We're setting off on our journey to the top, but on the way there will be some ladders for you to climb that will short-cut your progress so you get there even more quickly. How many ladders and where they'll be varies greatly from person to person – just keep your eyes open and lookout for them! There may be a few snakes to watch out for too. It's easy to avoid them by writing down your progress and measuring your success as you go. Then those pesky @(O_O)@ can't suck you back into their favourite downward spiral.

4. I often hear people say they aren't natural speakers or "It's OK for them, they were born that way!" While I tend to agree that there are personality types more attuned to speaking, I believe that once you know how to tame the monkeys, have the right mindset and the necessary skills, then all you need to do is practice, get (realistic) feedback and keep going and continue improving. I'm not saying that it will be a really fast journey to becoming a good presenter or speaker; after all it might take a while if you want to become famous, for example, but most of us just want to be great speakers, effective at getting our message across in a manner that motivates the audience and communicates our message in the desired manner.

Warning

✗   Disempowering beliefs aren't helpful – positive or at least neutral beliefs are.

✗   Learning that starts at the skills level often doesn't change behaviours. While you know HOW to do it you may still find yourself NOT DOING the new thing. Learning that starts at the level of motivation and beliefs ENCOURAGES PERMANANENT attitude and behaviour change and may feel "different" from other approaches.

✗   If you believe you hate speaking, learning new skills won't help much. You need to lose your fear and then learn new skills.

✗   Monkeys often prevent you from taking action. Reading the exercises is not enough – you need to *do* them!

✗   Monkeys prevent realistic feedback from reaching your brain (all too often overly negative feedback is taken in).

✗   If you don't read how to successfully complete the programme the monkeys might trip you up or trick you!

Key takeaways

✓ Making permanent change is easy – with all the right ingredients.

✓ Motivation is derived from your motives for learning – in this case what you want as a result of overcoming the monkeys.

o It is the energy to help you learn the process and overcome any small challenges along the way.

✓ Beliefs are things we think are true but aren't necessarily

o A negative monkey can be a disempowering belief about ourselves created unconsciously by an event in the past.

o A positive belief would be to believe that taming the monkeys process will be easy and effective.

✓ Skills are the actual things you need to know in order to learn.

o Be OK with using your imagination.

o Practical speaking skills are covered only once the monkeys are tamed.

✓ Taking action is essential – you'll need to do the exercises in order to experience the results.

✓ Feedback is a great ingredient as it provides you with the information you need to make sensible and reasonable changes to the course.

o There is no failure – only feedback.

Now you know how to have the best mindset for success, just hold that in your mind as I ask you to complete the exercises. If you feel the less helpful way cropping up, notice that and notice how a better mindset is more helpful. Remember, you're taking back charge of your own mind, no longer letting those @(O_O)@ have control! Let's get into the taming the @(O_O)@ process in more depth by first giving you an overview of the process in Chapter 4.

Chapter 4 –
The "Taming the monkeys" technique & case study

Taming the monkeys is all about filtering out those voices in your head that just create interference. It might sound abstract. But it isn't. Through the processes in this book you can get your @(O_O)@ working on your side and even turn them into voices of reason. Training your mind to deal rationally with fear is part of a complete solution, not just a one trick wonder. Any presenting fears are a thing of the past. I have worked with many hundreds of people (and their monkeys) and they all have similar experiences - either before they stand up to speak, as they are speaking or even after the talk...They hear little negative voices of self-doubt in their heads saying things like, *"You're rubbish", "You're going to mess up"* or *"What if they ask me a difficult question?"*.

Does any of that sound familiar? It's no wonder we can't always give great presentations when this sort of chatter is going on inside our heads, making us feel nervous and fearful! These voices then make us feel bad and that reflects in our body language and how we come across to others... That turns into a downward spiral.

Before you get to taming your own monkeys in the next chapter, I'll share with you a bird's eye view of the taming the monkeys technique, showing you step by step how the process works, using a fictitious client with real problems. We'll take an in-depth look at how she tamed her monkeys so you can see how the process could work for you. The monkeys are clever and very mischievous; they have plenty of tricks up their sleeves to try and throw you off track so take heed of my warnings and recommendations!

This chapter is structured a little like the game of charades – a guessing game where the players need to guess the title of a famous movie, book or play etc. The person acting it out can either act out the whole title in one like *"The Planet of the Apes"*, or they can work in smaller pieces acting the title out word by word. I am going to share the taming the monkeys process with you as both all in one and piece by piece. This chapter gives you an overview of it all in one. Then in the next chapter I'll take you step by step through the exercises you need to tame your monkeys completely.

The Three Golden Rules

By following the Three Golden Rules outlined in this book you'll rid yourself of presentation anxiety for good.

Golden Rule # 1: Catch Your Monkeys.

To catch the monkeys running around in your head you need to listen out for them. Don't ignore them. They won't just go away. Up until now that's probably what you've been told – to just ignore your fears. But that hasn't worked. Has it? So now it's time to do it differently and get a different result.

Golden Rule # 2: Connect With Your Monkeys.

Get to know the monkeys and understand why they're there. They are only trying to do what's best for you from their perspective based on the past, so tune in to the voices and hear what they're saying. The good, the bad and the downright ugly...

Golden Rule # 3: Challenge Your Monkeys.

This means you can decrease their power and hold over you. You no longer need to be fearful.

Don't worry, @(O_O)@ are all in your mind. Literally. So that means that when you learn to catch them, connect with them and challenge them, you'll be able to speak without anxiety and with real confidence.

Clients might not complete all of the process perfectly first time round but even a little progress starts to get them onto the upward spiral. Even a tiny bit of monkey taming begins the process of getting them on side. Then clients practise their techniques to get the @(O_O)@ working even more and more on their side. That way the results increase exponentially, in other words they totally blow their expectations away! But for now, let's focus on the first task: getting them on side. While reading through this example, begin to notice how you talk to yourself; what do those voices in your head say?

Case study – Taming your monkeys:

Case study - Golden Rule # 1: Catch Your Monkeys.

Catching your monkeys is the process whereby you listen to the voices in your head and begin to really hear what they are saying. Perhaps for the first time ever, the monkeys get to be heard.

At any point in the process from now until the process is complete, the client in this case, Georgie, might start to show emotions because she's starting to get in touch with her previously buried monkeys. Once she's confirmed she's medically fit to start this process, we make sure we complete it ASAP so any negative emotions can quickly change to positive feelings of achievement and freedom at the end of the session. Different people have different reactions, from laughing to crying; from blinding flashes of the obvious to deep realisations and insights. Whatever Georgie feels is perfectly fine as long as she's able to manage her emotions well and remain aware of them whilst also being aware of any impact on her motivation.

Medical warning:

Although I treat these processes light-heartedly in this book, they're still extremely powerful techniques. They must be used with respect and if you're aware of any previous treatments or interventions that might impact upon your ability to work with issues and emotions in the past or from your childhood, or are in any doubt as to your emotional wellbeing, you must consult with your medical doctor before progressing with the taming the monkeys process.

Q: Dee: LISTEN TO YOUR MONKEYS - WHAT ARE THEY SAYING?

A: GEORGIE: *"What if you mess it up?"*

Important note:

> ➢ "What if you mess it up?" Feels like a pretty "big picture" monkey because it can cover a lot of things. So we went more into more detail by asking what was underneath that monkey.

> ➢ We looked into whether it was made up of smaller, separate or more specific monkeys, and it was

Q; Dee: what is underneath the *"what if you mess it up"* monkey?

(Or you could ask "what specifically is the 'what if you mess it up' monkey saying?"

A: GEORGIE:

"What if you get your numbers wrong?"

"What if you get negative feedback?"

"What if you forget what to say?"

> "What if you
> mess it up?"

"What if you get your numbers wrong?"	"What if you get negative feedback?"	"What if you forget what to say? "

Important note:

> ➤ These were now separate issues so I knew we were on the right track. But I knew there was still another level to drill down into because at this level the monkeys still weren't as simple as they could be. Monkeys are often very simply and personally expressed.

> ➤ With each monkey you need to ensure that it passes the 4S checklist (More about this later!):

> ✓ Specific

> ✓ Separate

> ✓ Small

> ✓ Simple

Q: what is underneath "what if you get your numbers wrong?"

A: *"You're wrong"*

Q; what is underneath "what if you get negative feedback?"

A: *"You're wrong"*

Q: what is underneath "what if you forget what to say?"

A: *"You'll look stupid". Actually, that's: "you're stupid"*

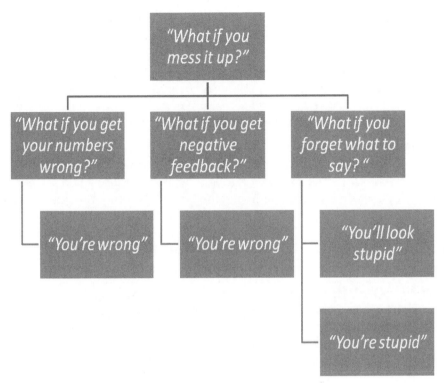

Important note:

> ➤ You must uncover the exact monkey words that are being used – the words or phrases they might repeat over and over. For example some people's monkeys might say, *"You're stupid"* and another person's monkeys might say, *"You'll never amount to anything".* While these might appear similar to some, in fact to the individual they*'re very different.* You'll get the best results when you identify the exact words that your monkeys say - however silly or out of date they may seem (and they probably will!)

> ➤ Monkeys often phrase things as *"You're..."* rather than *"I am...".* Notice how the two feel different

> ➤ After this process some clients may be feeling lower on the emotional scale as they get in touch with monkeys they haven't listened to for a while. That's OK as long as they're in charge of their emotional state. Moving on very quickly through the process will help. If this process was really easy everyone would have done it. I said it was simple - not that it's always easy!

> Many clients begin to feel so much better just by doing this one exercise - not because their fears have totally disappeared yet, but because the monkeys have become smaller and more manageable creatures. Many of them are just funny now. You might find it totally unbelievable that you actually took their comments on board! Some might disappear of their own accord just through realisation and self-awareness, but others will need to go through to the next step.

When you come to catch your personal monkeys I'll cover the process in more detail, but for now I just want to give you a general overview - a bird's eye view of the process. We're going to work through the examples using two of Georgie's monkeys that we've identified (although there are often more than two). So let's take a look at the second golden rule.

Case study - Golden Rule # 2: Connect With Your Monkeys.

Once all of the monkeys are down to their simplest and most personal form the next step is to connect with them. This involves uncovering why each monkey's there and what event or trigger in the past caused it to come about.

Important note:

> Before we connect with the @(O_O)@ it's important to understand their common traits in order to understand and connect with them effectively. In the next chapter we'll go through these in detail, but for now here's an overview of monkey traits:

1. Monkeys have your "best interests at heart" and (over) protect you

2. Each monkey has a personal life purpose e.g. to stop you repeating a "mistake"

3. Each monkey has its unique date of birth when a trigger event happened

4. Monkeys are out of date because they haven't been updated

5. Monkeys are over sensitive – they always take things too personally

6. Monkeys love to be drama queens - they love to blow things out of proportion

> In order to connect with the monkeys there are some set questions that Georgie just needs to answer off the top of her head. She might feel like she's guessing or making it up, but even guessing has to come from somewhere. Clients know when they've given the "right" answer and often it's not the answer you think you "should give"!

Connect with your monkey – example 1: "You're wrong" monkey

Dee: why would that @(O_O)@ (the "you're wrong" monkey) have come about? What's its life purpose? What's it trying to protect you from?

Georgie: *To protect me from making a mistake*

Dee: what age were you the very first time this feeling came about?

Georgie: *Three years old*

Dee: what event or trigger happened when you were three (perhaps at school or at home) that could have made the monkey think you had a problem - you didn't want to make mistakes?

Georgie: *I can't remember exactly but I have a feeling of my mum telling me off – shouting at me and telling me I was wrong*

At this point we've achieved what we need to at this step. We've connected with the original trigger for the "you're wrong" monkey – it was a point in time when Georgie was three when she felt her mum told her off.

Connect with your monkey – example 2: "You're stupid" monkey

Dee: why would that @(O_O)@ ("you're stupid" monkey) have come about? What's its life purpose? What's it trying to protect you from?

Georgie: *To help me avoid looking stupid in front of people*

Dee: what age were you the very first time this feeling came about?

Georgie: *About five years old*

Dee: what event or trigger happened when you were five (perhaps at school or at home) that could have made the monkey think you had a problem - that you didn't want to look stupid in front of people?

Georgie: *In junior school everyone else could read better than me. I had to stand up and read something but I couldn't do it properly; I didn't know how. The teacher called me "stupid" and all my friends laughed at me.*

We've connected with the original trigger for the "you're stupid" monkey – it was a point in time when Georgie was five when she remembered a teacher calling her stupid and all her friends laughing at her.

Important note:

> ➤ These actual memories may or may not be true, because 100% memories are pretty tricky to track, but that doesn't matter. What matters is that we've identified the VERY FIRST connection that caused the monkey to come about.

> ➤ Getting the first connection is also important because these events are likely to be smaller and less emotional for Georgie than if I ask her to remember just any event from her past – then it could be a more emotional event from later in life and we don't want to or need to go there!

> ➤ At this point in the process, clients' emotions may start to show. Sometimes the causes have been buried for so long that just uncovering them is emotional. Different people have different reactions - from laughing to crying. There are no *wrong* emotions; just ones that need to come out. But the key is that we don't feed the monkeys – the client and I remain aware of those emotions and move on quickly. We might use the confidence charm taught in the next chapter or other techniques to regain a useful emotional frame of mind for the next task.

Connect with your monkey – Traffic lights

The next step for Georgie was to rate her monkeys on a traffic light system which I'll explain fully in the next section - but for now it's enough to know that Red and Amber moneys are the ones that cause us problems and the Green monkeys are those that cause us problems and the Green monkeys are those that are helpful.

The "You're wrong" monkey is a Red monkey because it's false. The monkey's telling her everything or most things she does is wrong, but that's not true. That's why we class it as a Red monkey. If Georgie was running into a presentation with facts and figures but hadn't done enough preparation because it was all so last minute then the "You're wrong" monkey might be Amber. She exaggerates things but might nevertheless have a small point to make. For example she might be partly wrong because she didn't have time to check her numbers. But she might be right or it might be a small part of an otherwise great presentation. Perhaps Georgie could use the word "estimates" or "rough calculations" to cover the issue - that would make it an Amber monkey – exaggerated but with a tiny element of truth.

The "You're stupid" monkey is also a Red monkey because she isn't stupid - but the monkey insists that she is. She isn't stupid because she's got the role she is in; she isn't stupid or she wouldn't be asked to do the presentation; she isn't stupid because she knows so much about her subject. Can you see why these monkeys are so dangerous in a speaking situation? The last thing you need when you want to make a really important talk is for your monkeys to yell out "You're wrong!" or "You're stupid!".

Georgie rates both her monkeys as Red, and I agree.

We take forward the Red and Amber monkeys to be challenged using Golden Rule 3.

Any Green monkeys go on hold for now. We'll address them from Chapter 6 onwards because Green monkeys are likely to be about missing skills that you need to learn. For example, not knowing what to do with your hands when talking. That's fine because these Green @(O_O)@ aren't wild; they're just

**We take forward the Red and Amber monkeys to be challenged using Golden Rule 3.
Any Green monkeys go on hold for now.**

telling you about genuine skills you're lacking and that you can easily learn from great speakers.

Golden Rule # 3: Challenge Your Monkeys.

To challenge your Red and Amber monkeys you need to take the monkeys to court

Challenge your monkeys -"Taking the monkeys to court"

Example 1: "You're wrong"

The idea is that we're cross examining the monkey in a court of law, really getting down to the nitty gritty and seeing what evidence, if any, the monkey actually has to enable him to say these things. When we go through the process with Georgie you'll begin to notice how weak or non-existent the evidence is!

Let's look at what happened when Geoi I took the monkeys to court, starting wi "You're wrong " monkey.

DEE: How do you <u>know</u> **you're wroi**

GEORGIE: *Because I feel that way sometimes, I don't always get everything right*

DEE: If you took it to court, would the monkey have any <u>evidence</u> against you?

GEORGIE: *That time at the conference -when I said the wrong percentage in the introduction*

DEE: In court, what evidence do you have to the contrary? When have you **HAVEN'T been wrong**?

GEORGIE: *I suppose I'm not wrong every day at work. I'm right when I do my customer figures. I've done quite a few team meeting updates and they went well*

DEE: In what way is this monkey being ridiculous?

GEORGIE: I'm not often wrong and everyone's wrong sometimes. If I did make a mistake again I could just refer back to my notes anyway, correct myself and get back on track.

DEE: Would you say these things to your best friend?

GEORGIE: I suppose not because it's not very encouraging is it? Telling her all the time that she's wrong, it wouldn't do much for her self-confidence!

DEE: Have you considered that to be perfect, you need imperfections?

GEORGIE: *I suppose some people are forgiving if you make a mistake or don't get everything right all the time – they like to see a few flaws!*

DEE: (If the monkey had mentioned you're always wrong...) what do you mean **always?** What, every single time? **You're always wrong all of the time?**

GEORGIE: *No of course not. I've done several presentations before and it was OK then. I remembered my key numbers. I guess it just feels like I'm often wrong because I remember those times more!*

If Georgie had received some negative feedback in the past:

DEE: How many people said, **"You're wrong"**?

GEORGIE: *My boss told me once a few years ago in an appraisal - and of course that teacher*

DEE: How many people have never mentioned that **"You're wrong"**?

GEORGIE: *I suppose everyone else! Everyone who works with me, my customers and everyone who has listened to me present but haven't said anything, which must be hundreds!*

DEE: Has anyone said that **it went well/you're RIGHT**?

GEORGIE: *Lots of people said it went well. My colleagues always say I've done a good job and so do my customers so I must be doing something right.*

DEE: Why didn't you believe them? Do they often lie?

GEORGIE: *I suppose I never thought of it that way before – no I don't think they're lying! I guess I need to pay more attention to the positive feedback I received not just dwell on less positive comments from years ago!*

Example 2 "You're stupid"

DEE: How do you <u>know</u> **you're stupid**?

GEORGIE: *Because I never went to university; because my mum told me so; because I lost my place in the last presentation*

DEE: If you took it to court, would the monkey have any <u>evidence</u> against you?

GEORGIE: *I haven't got a degree. I did get a bit lost in my presentation last time*

DEE: In court, what evidence do you have to the contrary? When **HAVEN'T you been stupid**?

GEORGIE: *I work with numbers all day and I'm very quick so I know I'm not stupid. I just felt a little silly when I lost track of where I was during my presentation*

DEE: In what way is this monkey being ridiculous?

GEORGIE: *I only lost track that once, after I got the number wrong. It threw me a little bit. No one except me noticed I was lost. I suppose if I was clear on my structure and had easy to read notes I could easily get back on track.*

DEE: Would you say these things to your best friend?

GEORGIE: *No I'd never tell her she was stupid, of course not! That's rude and not polite! I don't think we'd stay friends for long! She's not stupid and even if she got a bit lost in what she was saying that doesn't make her stupid.*

DEE: Have you considered that to be perfect, you need imperfections?

GEORGIE: *I suppose now I think about it we all have them*

DEE: (If the monkey had said **"You're always stupid..."**) What do you mean **always?** What, every single time? **You're always stupid all of the time**?

GEORGIE: *No of course not. I'm not stupid! I've got a good job and I'm good at it. It just feels like I'm stupid sometimes when I do something wrong – but I know I'm not! Not having a degree doesn't make me stupid!*

If Georgie had received some negative feedback in the past:

DEE: How many people said, **"You're stupid"**?

GEORGIE: *No one, just me - and my mum that one time*

DEE: How many people have **never mentioned that "You're stupid"**?

GEORGIE: *I suppose everyone I know! All my work buddies, friends, people at church, neighbours... which must be a fair few!*

DEE: Has anyone said that **it went well/you're CLEVER**?

GEORGIE: *Lots of people say I'm good with numbers. They say they couldn't do it that quickly. My music teacher says I'm learning really quickly and picking it up well so if I was stupid I couldn't do that.*

DEE: Why didn't you believe them? Do they often lie?

GEORGIE: *I believe them now! I didn't hear their words properly before. I think the monkeys got in the way! I can see I'm not stupid - that's stupid!*

Important note:

> ➤ I will explain this in more detail in the next section before you tame your personal monkeys, but sometimes just seeing it in action is the best way to see the bigger picture and get a feel for how it works

> ➤ The questions are specifically designed to identify and then begin to loosen up less helpful beliefs and shake them around until the monkey's tamed

> ➤ Some of the questions will give huge realisations and change, or all of them may just slowly build up to a "change of mind"

> ➤ By the end of the questions Georgie was seeing things as they really were. She'd tamed her monkeys and was ready to build her skills

> ➤ The very process of questioning our monkeys' thoughts and beliefs allows us to feel differently about the event

> ➤ In each case we've learnt what the monkey wanted us to and we can now move on

In Chapter 5 I'll take you through the step by step the process so you can see what to look out for and how to tame your own monkeys easily and quickly like Georgie.

Having worked through each of her two monkeys, Georgie has tamed them. She knows she's "done" because she feels that the monkeys won't bother her anymore; she can talk about them but they won't have any hold on her or negative feelings connected to them. She might not be totally convinced yet, because she hasn't got up to speak, but the feeling is definitely that it's worked.

> **In Chapter 5, I'll take you through the step by step the process so you can see what to look out for and how to tame your own monkeys easily...**

The only emotion she might feel after this process is from Green monkeys. Because, Green monkeys want you to learn a specific skill so you can speak well. The only thing you then have to do is go ahead and learn that skill and lots of other beneficial skills which will be covered in Chapters 6,7, 8 and 9 - or you can follow the "Next Steps" advice in Chapter 10 to find any other answers you need.

Helpful hints to make it even easier to tame the monkeys

Now you've seen how Georgie and I would work together to tame the monkeys I want to cover a few suggestions I have on how to get the best from the process

Recruit some support - a public speaking buddy

Some people find it easier and more fun with a monkey buddy. Some people prefer working alone and others prefer sharing their experiences. This book has been designed to work with or without a buddy so either way it will work for you.

Some of the reasons I suggest people get someone to help them with the taming the monkeys process are:

> ➢ Having a buddy can help ease the challenges
>
> ➢ Asking someone to be your buddy demonstrates commitment to achieving your goal
>
> ➢ They can see things from an unbiased point of view. A part of you believes the monkeys are fibbing but there may be a part of you that believes they're speaking the truth, so your buddy can help you keep things in perspective
>
> ➢ They're less likely to fall for monkey tricks

A buddy will help you through the programme and support you along the way. I've written a note for you to show them. You may want to use it to make it even easier for them to understand what's involved and persuade them to help you.

Some people ask how best to go about getting a buddy - so here's what I suggest:

- List the traits of the type of person you want to consider, for example:
  - ✓ Someone who'll hold you accountable to answering their questions
  - ✓ Someone you trust and know has the best intentions for you at heart

    ✓ Someone kind enough to encourage you and ask questions in the right manner

    ✓ Someone strong enough to make sure that you do answer the questions and don't charm your way out of an answer!

- Make a list of who you could work with from a social or business group

- Consider who else has similar goals and might also like to tame their monkeys

  o If you're both doing the programme you can learn from one another

  o You might consider your buddy to be loads better than, or not as good as you. That's OK because monkey taming's an ongoing skill that can always do with a polish up, especially for those who continue to push their personal boundaries

- Think about who might be happy to help even if they aren't doing it themselves

  o They don't even need to know anything about speaking – they just need to follow the instructions to the exercises with you

- Ask them to help using the note below

A note to a potential monkey buddy

Dear monkey buddy,

Thank you very much for considering helping this person to tame their Public Speaking Monkeys® (Those voices people get inside their heads telling them they're rubbish or that they can't speak in public).

By the way, I should explain that I use the following visual shorthand to describe Public Speaking Monkeys®:

(Because the symbols look a bit monkey-like and it's shorter!)

It may have taken a lot for this person to ask you for help, so please bear with them if they seem a little apprehensive or not totally comfortable.

The exercises and questions throughout this programme have been specifically designed to go deep into the person's mind, uncover the monkey inside and expose its fibs and negative voices. Any questions and sentences are designed and constructed to unravel the monkey arguments. That's why it's important to stick to the exact words in the questions.

If you choose to accept the assignment then your job's just to follow the instructions. You don't really need to do anything much - in most situations monkey buddies don't say anything other than ask the questions or help them through the exercises in order. Of course you don't need to know the answers - we aren't asking *you* to answer them and they aren't your monkeys! Please don't go "off piste" because that could undo some of the good work.

The best attitude you can have is a supportive, yet firm and strong one. Don't buy into their problems and start talking about them, just nicely bring them back on topic and encourage them to answer the question. You might need to ask it several times before they realise you aren't going to let them get away with avoiding it.

A buddy is sometimes key when the monkeys are so mischievous that they trick the person reading the book. They try to stop them from answering the questions properly. The person really wants to sort the pesky monkeys out but if the monkeys sense that their current habitat's under threat they might manipulate that person into avoiding the questions. It's amazing how many excuses and reasons some people and their monkeys create to avoid answering and challenging the monkeys:

- I don't have time to do it now

- I'm not in the mood

- If I get stroppy I can ignore the question

They come up with these even though they know that as they begin to answer the questions the monkeys' power diminishes! Your job then is to encourage your partner, lend a helping hand and get them to answer the relevant questions for each exercise or monkey.

Humour may be helpful when getting rid of @(O_O)@ - but you must only use it to laugh at some of the @(O_O)@ beliefs and exaggerations, NOT at the person.

If you're going to use humour, use it with forethought and compassion but please do go ahead and use it.

Once the person themselves realises how stupid some of the things the @(O_O)@ say and believe are - it becomes much easier to let those old beliefs and monkeys go. Allow the person to come to that conclusion themselves. Also hold in your mind that it's not the monkeys that are stupid -they thought they were protecting the person at the time - it's some of their conclusions, generalisations and exaggerations that might be amusing.

Just guide your person through the exercises and help them to answer and record their thoughts in their workbook. If you've chosen to do the programme too, good for you! You can progress through the chapters together, and when it comes to actually doing the taming the monkey process then you must complete the whole thing all at once and then swap around (rather than doing each golden rule and swapping around which would leave each person a little in limbo and not in the best frame of mind to help the other one).

Thanks

Dee Clayton – Public Speaking Monkey Trainer and Tamer

Key takeaways

- ✓ There are three golden rules in the taming the monkeys process
  - o Golden Rule # 1: Catch Your Monkeys
  - o Golden Rule # 2: Connect With Your Monkeys
  - o Golden Rule # 3: Challenge Your Monkeys
- ✓ Catching - Georgie's underneath monkeys were "You're wrong" and "You're stupid"
- ✓ Connecting – we uncovered each event or trigger that caused the monkeys to arise
  - o Monkey by monkey we identified the event
  - o The monkeys were graded using the traffic light system
- ✓ Challenging - you saw the taking the monkeys to court technique in which Georgie challenged her monkeys and thus neutralised them.

✓ Recruiting a public speaking buddy can make it even easier to tame your monkeys

   o   Use the note provided to help explain the buddy's roles and responsibilities

> **We cover the three steps in a lot more detail in this next chapter, which should also answer any questions you might have.**

Now Georgie has tamed her monkeys she knows how to overcome her presenting anxiety. Now it's your turn. You may want to read the next chapter through to get the general feel and then actually do the exercises writing your answers on the second sweep. However you choose to go ahead, ensure that before you start the live process you have enough time to go all the way through until the monkeys are tamed. This might take 10 minutes or several hours depending on your ability to communicate well with yourself, to manage your emotions and to trust in the process.

We cover the three steps in a lot more detail in this next chapter, which should also answer any questions you might have – so, over to you!

Chapter 5 –
Your turn to Tame your Monkeys

Not all @(O_O)@ are "bad" but those causing you trouble are the ones that are a little bit wild and need taming. The aim of this process is either to get rid of all the wild monkeys or tame and train them to become supportive and helpful monkeys instead — because they can be good and helpful too (you may have some of those already). "Good monkeys" are often quieter and don't cause trouble so you're often less aware of them as they whisper positive or neutral things in your ears.

The problem with the "bad" monkeys is that if you believe their disempowering mutterings you've already decided how the presentation's going to go before you even start. Haven't you? You THINK it's going to be a disaster. You've imagined turning up, falling over the wires, getting muddled, forgetting your words, faces like thunder and just when you think it's all over you get asked that very question you know you can't answer. You've already imagined the whole event before you've even thought about what to say!! That's why it's time to get these cheeky little monkeys under control.

If you don't tame your monkeys there's no way you can get them to behave as you wish long-term. Sure, you might be able to temporarily tempt them into behaving in a certain way; you might be able to teach them new tricks so that occasionally they can do one thing or another, but if you want it to become a natural learned behaviour that your monkeys are on your side, you need to tame them. Once they're no longer wild animals and they are tamed you have control over them, rather than them over you.

> **Not all @(O_O)@ are "bad" but those causing you trouble**
> **are the ones that are a little bit wild and need taming.**
> **The aim of this process either to get rid of all the wild**
> **monkeys or tame and train them**
> **to become supportive...**

This chapter is where <u>you</u> complete the taming the monkeys process yourself.

Let's remind ourselves of the three steps involved with monkey taming:

Golden Rule # 1: Catch Your Monkeys.

To catch the monkeys running around in your head you need to listen out for them.

Golden Rule # 2: Connect With Your Monkeys.

Get to know the monkeys and understand why they're there. Tune in to the voices and hear what they're saying. The good, the bad and the downright ugly...

Golden Rule # 3: Challenge Your Monkeys.

This means you can decrease their power and hold over you.

At any stage in the process the monkeys can disappear totally or become tamed as you adjust and remove the pathways in your mind that make you feel nervous.

Also, at any point in the process you may notice different emotions as you start to get in touch with the previously buried monkeys. You might feel like laughing, crying or experience deep realisations and insights. Wherever your reaction it's perfectly fine as long as you remain aware of your emotions and the potential impact it can have upon motivation!

When we experience less positive emotions it's less simple to stay on the upward spiral and easier to fall for the monkeys tricks. For that reason I ask you do several things to protect yourself:

1. Read through the chapter once without doing the exercises. Before most of the exercises there is a preparation or teaching section explaining everything you need to know before you sail smoothly through the exercises following the instruction. It is best that you read all of those preparation and teaching sections first and then you can go through this chapter again, concentrating on gliding through the exercises easily.

2. Once you've started the live process of going through the exercises, you'll want to make sure you complete it quickly all the way through without interruptions — unless you have any serious cause to stop. This will:

   a. Prevent you falling onto or getting stuck on a downward spiral

   b. Stop you and your buddy from being tempted to feed your monkeys

   c. Mean you don't fall for any monkey tricks and traps

   d. Help you move quickly past any less positive emotions

Once you start the process, don't stop (except for comfort breaks of course!) Log your answers in your workbook.

3. If you're working with a monkey buddy, do one complete live process with one person before swapping around and doing it with the other person. Ensure you allow enough time to complete the process.

4. Make sure you've completed the questions in Chapter 3 thoughtfully

   It is important to have completed the goal-setting exercises earlier on in case your motivation doesn't remain high. The monkeys are very clever and try plenty of tricks to stop you catching them. One of their best tricks is to de-motivate you so you say things like:

   a. *It's not important right now — I'll leave it till later*

   b. *This won't work for me even though I've not tried yet!*

   c. *I won't finish reading the book or get to the end*

   d. *I can't do it so why bother anyway*

5. If the going gets tough either now or later it's your motivation and goals that will see you through. This is where your answers to the questions in Chapter 3 need to be big enough to provide "motive-ation" for you.

6. Having booked in the time to complete the process will also help you to stick to schedule. If you find yourself questioning your motivation and not being totally sure that you want to do all the steps and exercises as instructed in this book then open your eyes. See the mischievous traps they want you to fall into and lean on your motivation to see you through to the end.

7. Ensure you are emotionally fit to complete the process

   Medical warning: The techniques I am about to share are extremely powerful. They must be used with respect and only with positive intentions – to rid yourself (or your buddy) of the public speaking monkeys holding them back. If you've had any previous treatments or interventions that might be related to, or impact upon, your ability to work with issues and emotions from your childhood or past or if you're in any doubt as to your emotional wellbeing you MUST consult with your medical doctor before proceeding with the taming your monkeys process. Please note my advice is not medical advice.

8. Create and use your personal confidence charm

    Before we start on the golden rules, I want to show you how to create a confidence charm. You only need to create it once and then you can use it at anytime over and over when you need an emotional lift. It's not a total solution but it's a good "quick fix" to see you through any challenging times and help ensure you remain on the upward spiral. I thought it was important to give you this tool here so that you have several ways to distract the monkeys if you need to throughout the process.

Exercise: Create a personal confidence charm

a) If you have a buddy this is a great exercise to discuss and do together. If not, no worries, just find a quiet space and use your imagination.

b) Think back to a time when you felt really confident. It can be in any situation when you felt confident – from childhood or recently. From work, at home or in a hobby. It really doesn't matter where you felt the confidence — people I've worked with have used baking, horse-riding, running and even DIY as their areas of confidence.

c) As you remember back to that specific time, where in your body was that feeling of confidence? How did it feel? Look around you. What can you see as you feel really confident? Listen, what can you hear?

d) Adapt your body position to make yourself feel even more confident. Try sitting up straight or standing.

e) When you feel really confident and before the feeling reduces, you're ready to "lock and load" the feeling and store it in your mind by "tagging" it. To add a physical tag, gently press your thumb and middle finger together on your left hand as you think about being really confident. Separate the thumb and finger when the peak of that feeling has just started to fade.

f) Change the subject for a second to take your mind off that one example and then repeat steps b) to e) at least three times using different examples, of times when you felt confident or capabable of anything.

g) Test the charm by pressing the same thumb and finger together on your left hand and that feeling of confidence will begin to develop inside you. If you need to add more powerful memories, keep repeating the process.

h) Some of you will find this easier than others as we have different levels of confident memories. If you aren't finding it easy to remember a time when you were confident then just imagine or make up an event and *pretend* to be confident. How would you be standing? How would you look? See that image in your mind's eye, ensuring that in the image you're looking through your own eyes (rather than seeing a picture of yourself doing it).

i) In addition, every time you feel confident in real life you can tag that feeling onto your confidence charm by pressing the same thumb and finger together again and releasing after the peak.

j) Any time you feel you need a confidence boost — fire off this confidence charm by pressing your thumb and middle finger on your left hand together for a few moments and the feeling of confidence will come.

This charm isn't the whole thing and you may find it easy or not – it's just another little tool to help you build your confidence and manage your emotions. Use your confidence charm, positive thoughts, uplifting music, favourite poems, monkey buddies or any number of positive thoughts to help you hop off the downward spiral or cling onto the upward one for dear life!

"Monkey Tail"

I find even when I do something I enjoy and want to do, such as playing sport or getting up early for a holiday flight, there can still be some initial inertia or negative emotion such as "I don't want to go" or "Perhaps I can lie in bed just a little longer!".Once I've actually done it, though, I'm always glad I have and enjoyed it! So if there's a little resistance even to things we like doing it's normal that there may be a little inertia related to taming your monkeys. Yes it's something we want to do but it's not quite the same as going on holiday is it?

1) How to Catch your PUBLIC SPEAKING MONKEYS®

Think of @(O_O)@ as wild animals. If you wanted to tame them you'd first have to catch them right? Well that's true of @(O_O)@. Often people are so used to @(O_O)@ being there that they don't find it totally easy to catch them. That may be because they're so used to ignoring them that they can't find them... They might be surrounded by them and so used to it, they're almost blind to their presence.

As we saw in Georgie's case study, taming them was firstly about discovering what the monkey voices were saying. So let's get to know these fellas better and listen to what they have to say.

A. Listen to the monkeys

Don't ignore them – see what they say to you.

Most people get taught to ignore their monkeys. Sometimes, to learn to listen to them, you'll need to ignore or disregard what you've learnt in the past. Often clients have been told to just ignore problems. You may have mentioned your fear of speaking before and someone else said to you, "Just ignore it!" or "Get over it!".

Many people ignore them, hide them and bury their heads in the sand, so to speak, hoping they'll go away. But they won't. I mean they haven't, have they? Has that worked for you? I'm guessing not if you're following this programme. You haven't yet managed to shut up the monkeys in your head.

Now, I know what you're thinking: there may have been the odd occasion when you did manage to keep them quiet long enough for you to present, but did it work long term or did they just pop up twice the size next time?

Some clients tell me they've been given alternative ways to "deal "with the problem; they may have been told to "picture the audience naked" — well, rather you than me! I'm not sure the picturing a whole room of 80 people naked is the best way to approach a presentation — especially an important presentation. I think it might put me off to be honest. Apart from that I don't even want to begin to imagine what your body language is unconsciously saying to the audience with that on your mind! (More on body language later).

If you ignore the monkeys they don't tend to go away. Monkeys exist to tell you about a problem... When you hide them under the carpet they just multiply and get worse and worse and worse and sometimes come out at just the wrong time — when you really wanted to give an amazing presentation. What happens when the monkeys are under the carpet is boredom. They run around causing havoc and become even more wild and difficult to catch. When they meet other monkeys, they learn new tricks from one another and start to plot ways to escape the carpet prison! Listen, if ignoring the monkeys hasn't worked yet then it's important to do something different!

"Monkey Tail"

Everyone I've met gets the monkeys at some point. A long time ago as I was perfecting the monkey technique, I worked with a group of senior managers. The brief was "Advanced Presentation Skills". These people presented frequently and so I didn't know if they would experience monkeys or not. I took them through the concept and everyone told me they didn't get monkeys. This was the first time I'd presented the concept to such experienced presenters and so, foolishly, I believed them and skipped the monkey section to go ahead and have more time teaching the advanced skills.

Unfortunately on day two of the course, when they knew they had to do a time-pressured final presentation pulling together all of the new approaches and advanced elements that had been taught... yes, you guessed it, the monkeys paid all of them a visit.

Perhaps they didn't believe they had monkeys, or perhaps they were too worried to talk about them in front of colleagues, but from that experience I learnt a lot. Now I believe that everyone has some kind of monkey sometimes and if they aren't stretching themselves enough to be experiencing the moneys right now I turn up the pressure so that they can start to see where their personal monkey limit is. If they're comfortable with a room of 20, what about 200? What about 2000? If they're OK talking to colleagues what about world experts?

B. Separate the monkeys

Once you begin to listen to the monkeys inside you then need to <u>hear each one separately</u>. Clients tell me when I first work with them that there are often lots of monkeys all speaking at once so it's not easy to hear what they're saying. If you just let them chatter away all speaking at once you can't possibly deal with them.

It's a bit like being in a meeting where everyone's talking at the same time. Instead of hearing everyone's point of view you actually end up missing out on what everyone's saying and not getting anywhere!

By going through the process of separating them you'll be able to identify with each monkey one at a time, acknowledge their presence and give each monkey the attention that it deserves.

C. Drill down to the "underneath monkey"

We now need to do a second sweep of the monkey list to make sure none are cleverly hiding away. We need to drill down on them enough to ensure we've totally "caught" each individual one and none are cheekily hiding trying to avoid capture. The 4S Checklist will help you to avoid falling for the monkeys' clever ways and help you to identify the main monkeys and, after work on them, to get the biggest and best result!

4S Monkey Checklist – Are your monkeys Specific Separate, Small and Simple?

With each monkey you need to ensure that it is:

- o   Specific

- o   Separate

- o   Small

- o   Simple

Specific – give enough detail so that others could understand the monkey

We need to check that the monkeys you've written down are detailed. That way you can identify the specific problem. We're looking for a real problem that you could explain to someone you didn't know and in a way they'd easily understand. For example someone might write that one of their monkeys is *"You're going to get nervous"*. This is indeed a monkey but you could argue it's not a specific monkey yet. It's difficult to explain to another person what you mean by nervous without getting more specific and separating out the different elements of that monkey.

Separate – disconnect the monkeys from one another

The *"You're going to get nervous"* monkey has not separated itself out yet into smaller monkeys.

You can tell there are smaller monkeys because "nervous" can mean many things to many people. You need to get to the smaller monkeys that often hideaway (avoiding capture) behind the bigger monkey — so ask the monkey!

Monkey, what do you mean by *"You're going to get really nervous?"*

Perhaps it will answer, *"You'll get sweaty palms"* or *"You'll be breathing too quickly"* or perhaps *"You're gonna start to shake".* Those are three specific and separate monkeys, which is what we're aiming for. Then each one can be worked on easily later on when we come to connect with the monkeys.

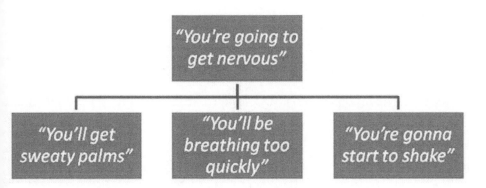

Small – the smaller the monkey the easier it will be to tame

The aim is to get to smaller monkeys rather than a few bigger monkeys. Your job is to find them and uncover them and notice that as you begin to identify the smaller monkeys some of the level of fear decreases too.

For example, the *"What if you mess it up?"* monkey seems like a huge problem to many of my clients, but when broken down into its smaller monkeys it begins to seem more manageable:

"What if you get your numbers wrong?"

"What if you get negative feedback?"

"What if you lose your place?"

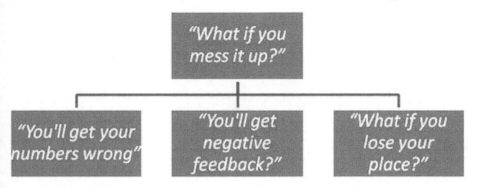

Simple- Monkeys use simple child-like language

You'll also want to make sure you've got to the simplest form of the smaller monkey – just ask yourself if what you've written down is simple. The monkeys we want to catch don't use complicated sentences used by adults. They speak as if they were children, using very simple and very child-like language — always look for simple and personal sentences.

In the previous example the smaller monkeys still seem quite grown up in their language e.g. *"You'll get your numbers wrong."*

If you need a tip for doing this, just go inside and ask each monkey individually...

"What's the simpler personal monkey underneath?" Or "What's the deeper worry or concern underneath that monkey?"

Top Tip: Underneath monkeys love repeating sayings or phrases they've heard before

Monkeys can also be a phrase or a saying. For example:

"You've got a brain like a sieve"

"You'll never amount to anything"

"You're shy"

For many people monkeys can depend on the context or environment you find yourself in. As you did the exercises above, you may have found that in different situations your response changed. Perhaps when you thought about presenting one to one that was OK, but when you think of standing up to talk to a group of customers the fears kick in? Previous clients have said their monkeys have screamed louder even in response to all sorts of environmental or external factors such as:

- More people in the room
- Increased seniority
- Friends or family present
- Need to talk about numbers and data
- Outside your specialist area
- Never done it before
- Need to use technology
- Need to talk about yourself
- Selling
- Explaining complex ideas

- Giving someone else's presentation

- Doing it in a different language

- Last minute

- Not having practised

- Not knowing where you will be presenting

If you notice this, just continue to follow the Catching the Monkey process — it will work just as well, as demonstrated in the visual shown:

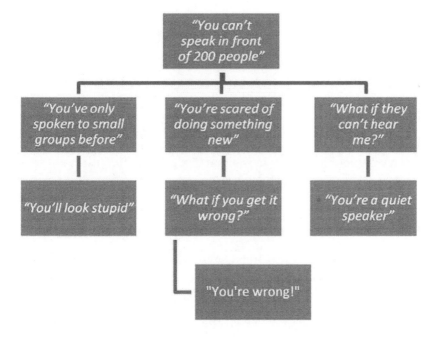

As you start the process of decreasing your fear of public speaking you can look forward to the journey. Look forward to being rid of your fear, knowing that you need to overcome a few challenges along the way. Having a buddy can help ease the challenges. There will be times when you're feeling proud and perhaps times when you even feel a little silly – that's OK and that's why it's light-hearted. When you make that connection and realise some of the fears are only very old and out of date beliefs stuck in your head, I bet some of them will make you smile.

Exercise – Catching your monkeys

1. Pick an appropriate occasion to allow yourself sometime to think about the monkeys, and actually write down what they're saying. If you have a buddy this is a great exercise to get one person to ask the questions and write down the exact answers while you just get to think and really listen to the @(O_O)@.

2. Write every single one down, no matter how scary or silly you think they are. It may take a little while to get in touch with them or it may be immediate, depending how well you've hidden them away.

3. As you hear the little voices, begin to listen to them. Ask them to speak one at a time if there are too many at once. Now go ahead and write yours down.

4. As a general rule, the ones you really want to avoid and not write down or admit to are the exact ones you need to write down and admit to! There are only correct answers so don't over-think it and do it as quickly as possible, allowing the monkeys to flow from your mind onto the page.

5. Review your list briefly to see that you've separated them out as much as you can. Check the monkeys are separate and then drill-down on each monkey to make sure you've identified the main monkeys to work with. It will be time well spent and it will make the rest of the process even easier and the results even more powerful.

6. If like many people you find it only too easy to hear the monkey voices, just listen to them at an appropriate time, write them down and then move directly on to the next section.

7. If you don't find it easy to hear them, then read the script below to get you into the "public speaking mood". Once you've completed the exercise, snap yourself out of that mood by looking up to the ceiling, saying *"Yes, yes, yes!"* to yourself and putting a big smile on your face. Notice how it positively changes your mood *now*.

    Optional: Script to get you into the "public speaking mood"

    If it isn't easy to get in touch with how you may be feeling when you get the monkeys then imagine this scenario.... You've just bumped into someone you work with — they tell you they have to rush out to visit an important client with a serious issue, but they're also due to give a presentation to a room full of 80 customers in five minutes. They shove their notes and presentation in your hand and run off out shouting, "Thanks for doing the presentation!". You stand there in shock and fear, wondering what to do next as those familiar monkey voices start to pay you a visit...

Now does this scenario help you to get in touch with your emotional levels better? Or imagine your own version of a nightmare presentation scenario. You only need to do that for as long as it takes to write down your monkeys.

Well done for writing your monkeys down. Remember that once you've gone through the process a few times it becomes much quicker and easier. The process of writing their words down acknowledges them and means you're really listening to what they say.

It really doesn't matter how many you have, but it is important to aim to catch them all. Some of them may seem really small, some very silly, some embarrassing but, whatever, they all need to be written down so you can deal with them effectively.

It really doesn't matter how many you have, but it is important to aim to catch them all. Some of them may seem really small, some very silly, some embarrassing but, whatever, they all need to be written down so you can deal with them effectively.

You've probably heard the saying that identifying the problem is the first step to resolving it? Well it's true, isn't it? As you begin to write down the monkeys some may start to disappear on their own because you start to verbalise them and realize how untrue some of them are. That's a good thing and it ensures you still continue with the process through to the end anyway. Otherwise you might find you've only half dealt with them and they could return.

"Monkey Tail"

A business woman came to me asking me to help her overcome her fear of speaking in public. When we started to work on "catching the monkeys" she initially thought she just had the one monkey but when we got going and got rid of the biggest one we uncovered many smaller ones lurking underneath.

There turned out to be a whole bunch of different monkeys muttering in her head, but she didn't find it easy to get in touch with them all straight away because her "I'm no good at speaking in public" monkey was shouting so loudly!

It doesn't matter if you think you have one and discover you have loads or you just have a few small ones to work with. The process is the same and it still works.

Exercise – Uncovering the "underneath monkey"

1. Review all the monkeys you wrote down in the previous exercise and keep writing the "underneath monkey" — acknowledging and really listening to what they say. *(Or if you find it easier ask "what specifically is the 'what if you ....' monkey saying?"*This is intended to be a progressive process — keep going to get to the underneath monkeys, asking yourself if anything more can be uncovered by separating the*m out.*

2. *The constant change and re-evaluation of what the monkeys say is part of the proces*s working already, so embrace it.

3. Check that you've completed this exercise by noticing that all your monkeys are expressed in the 4S format , that is:

    a. *Specific – gives enough detail so that others could understand the monkey*

    b. *Separate – each monkey is disconnected from the other monkeys, thus decreasing their power*

    c. *Small – You have identified each smaller monkey, which may still be a big concern for you, but will be easier to tame*

    d. *Simple – You've drilled down to simple child-like expressions of the concerns or worries.*

4. If you're working with a buddy, ask them to check that all your monkeys have passed the 4S checklist. Sometime it's easier for a buddy to see through any monkey traps!

5. It really doesn't matter how many you have, but it is important to aim to catch them all. Some of them may seem really small, some very silly, some embarrassing, but whatever you find they all need to be listed down so you can deal with them effectively.

Brilliant job! Well done for writing your monkeys down and spending the time looking at them in more detail.

As you wrote down the @(O_O)@ some may have started to disappear on their own because you've started to verbalise them and realize how untrue some of them are. That's a good thing — but continue with the process through to the end as well (otherwise you may find you've only half-dealt with them).

> **As you wrote down the @(O_O)@ some may have started to disappear on their own because you've started to verbalise them and realize how untrue some of them are.**

Some people may notice that some of the monkeys are related – like little monkey families! Perhaps the "What if they don't like me" monkey feels related to the "What if they think I'm boring?" monkey. That's perfectly OK. The important thing is to write everything down. What you might find later is that once you get rid of the one monkey, other related monkeys disappear too. You won't know until we get to Golden Rule #3: Challenging the Monkeys. So for now, just ensure that you've written them all down, no matter how similar or different they may appear.

If you don't find the process easy immediately and wonder if you are doing it right, that's OK because even a tiny bit of monkey taming begins the process of slowing or stopping them from working against you. If you haven't got it right you'll notice later and be able to revisit what those one or two monkeys are saying, so for now do your best and continue with the process. Don't let the "What if I'm not doing it right, what if it's not perfect, what if I'm wrong" monkeys paralyze you into inaction – move forward and do the next step!

Great. You now know how to follow Golden Rule 1 – Catch the Monkeys. You have a good grasp on the technique involved with:

A. Listening to the monkeys

B. Using the 4S format with your monkeys

C. Drilling down to the "underneath monkey"

It's actually quite simple once you know how to do it, so well done for sticking with it and learning that process. You can now use it forever!

It's well worth just re-scoring your confidence scale from earlier on to see if you've started to improve and score higher in your confidence already.

Next you're now ready to learn Golden Rule #2 -Connecting with the Monkeys. Each monkey that you've listed in this chapter is there for a reason. This is the basis of Golden Rule #2, so let's find out why they're there. And then more importantly why it's totally OK for them to leave now.

2) How to connect with the PUBLIC SPEAKING MONKEYS®

Now you know how to catch the monkeys they're no longer a faceless huge jungle — they're individual monkeys you can communicate with. You may have already begun to disconnect with some of them, or let their hold over you loosen as you begin to see and understand what's going on inside.

A bit like taming wild animals; just catching them isn't enough – you need to understand how they think and work in order to connect with them. By continuing with our journey and discovering how to connect with the monkeys we make a deep connection with the monkeys BEFORE we make any changes.

Understanding the monkeys

As we begin to connect with the @(O_O)@ it's important to see that they aren't trying to be evil, mean or vindictive. They've genuinely got your best interests at heart — even though it doesn't always feel that way! Having studied wild @(O_O)@ for years, I've noticed some common traits that are important for you to acknowledge in order to understand them better. So let's take a closer look at each one in turn.

1. *Monkeys have your "best interests at heart"*

   - All @(O_O)@ without exception believe they're doing the best by you (though that doesn't mean they are)!

   - Monkeys were originally just trying to look out for your wellbeing. (A bit like a caring friend or protective mum wanting to make sure you stay safe)

   - Their objective is either to protect you from something or to hide something away. But, as we know, in the long term their approach doesn't work

2. *Each monkey has a personal life purpose*

   - Each @(O_O)@ was born because of a specific event and therefore it has a specific purpose for existing. A significant part of the connecting process is understanding and appreciating each monkey's life purpose

   - It may be big or small — size is irrelevant. The important thing is to connect enough with each monkey so you can understand its sole purpose. It's likely for example that a @(O_O)@ might have a purpose of helping you to avoid "making the same mistake again"

3. *Each monkey has its unique date of birth*

   - Every monkey was born because of a specific event, on a specific date. The monkey was born to "protect you" from that event. Let's look at some examples which could have triggered a monkey's birth:

   - Someone saying something negative to you (e.g. a teacher saying you're stupid)

   - Hearing something you didn't like (e.g. your parents arguing)

   - Seeing something you didn't like (e.g. a look of disappointment when something wasn't "perfect")

   - Feeling a certain way that didn't feel nice (e.g. embarrassed in front of children in the classroom)

4. *Monkeys are often out of date*

   - Monkeys remember everything you've ever heard, seen, felt and noticed since they were born- often remembering more than you do consciously! These deep memories may have been stored away for so long you think you haven't remembered them, but of course the monkeys are part of you so you'll remember them if you want to when you're asked the right questions

   - Because our memories have stored them away for so long, they're likely to be out of date. It's a bit like running a 20 or 30 year-old version of software – can you imagine that? This process enables you to update your mind with the most current version and break free from the time warp

5. *Monkeys always take things too personally*

   - Naturally monkeys are very self-absorbed. They tend to believe that everything's about them

   - Monkeys never look around to understand their surroundings or the other people involved, so they often misunderstand the situation or become confused

   - Because it's "all about them", they also have a tendency to think everything's their fault. If an audience member is yawning or looking tired it must because you're boring. (It couldn't possibly be that they have jet lag, having travelled eight hours to get to the international conference!)

- Everything you've ever said to yourself or others, everything you've seen or heard — they take it all personally. For example even if you've ever seen someone else make a mistake and you felt bad for them, a new-born monkey may have popped up and jumped into action to protect you from making the same mistake. Even though it wasn't you that made the "mistake" in the first place!

6. *Monkeys love to be drama queens*

- Even if the monkeys aren't confused and they've got exactly the right message, they do have a tendency to blow things out of proportion. They just love being the drama queen — making things appear so much worse than they actually are. If an audience member's using their phone to text during your talk @(O_O)@ might tell you it's a "*disaster*" and it must be because they "*hate your presentation*"! But maybe they're just texting their child who's asked to be picked up earlier than expected

- It's a way to get attention — so if you give them attention in another way (through this process) they'll learn over time that they no longer have to play the drama queen role!

Exercise – *Connecting with your monkeys*

It is now time to connect with the monkeys as if they were best friends, to really understand their point of view. Why were they born? What's their life purpose? What's the thing they're trying to protect you from?

Instead of telling them off or ignoring them as we may have done most of our lives, now's our chance to befriend them and understand things from their perspective. The trick is not to agree with them, not to get sucked into their drama queen world where everything's so terrible, but to empathise and understand why they may have felt like they did. At the very least you'll want to appreciate that they were only trying to protect you and do their best for you. Then we'll move on to taming them and quietening them down, but the only job to focus on for now is understanding without getting sucked in! Just realising that some of these monkeys are so out of date is part of the taming process.

Exercise – Uncover your triggers and @(O_O)@ positive intention for you.

This exercise is about helping you to connect with your @(O_O)@. The aim is to find the original event that caused a problem and then understand what the monkey was trying to protect you from. Write the answers in your workbook because tracking them is important and will enable you to see your improvements through the programme.

Uncover on your own or with your buddy what the original event was that started each monkey off on their trip to the wild side. Ask yourself or your buddy the questions below

1. WHY WOULD THAT @(O_O)@ HAVE COME ABOUT?

2. WHAT'S ITS LIFE PURPOSE?

3. WHAT'S IT TRYING TO PROTECT YOU/ME FROM?

4. WHAT AGE WERE YOU/WAS I THE VERY FIRST TIME THAT FEELING CAME ABOUT?

    a. You just need to uncover the approximate age you were when the monkey was born. It doesn't need to be exact, but often it is

    b. As long as your answer is during your childhood and probably under the age of seven you're likely to be on the right track

    c. Many clients say they don't know, and that's fine – just guess, because guesses have to come from somewhere and it might just be your inner mind. When you go with the flow it will begin to work so let go and try it — you have everything to gain and only monkeys to lose!

5. WHAT EVENT OR TRIGGER HAPPENED WHEN YOU WERE/I WAS (age)... PERHAPS AT SCHOOL OR AT HOME THAT COULD HAVE MADE THE MONKEY THINK YOU/I HAD A PROBLEM? (re-state problem)

    a. If you need to just guess at the answers, go ahead – it will still work! Write down all your answers to the question however silly they may seem

    b. Don't over analyse this exercise – just run with it and see what comes up. If you try too hard to get the "right" answer it can be off-putting, so go with the flow!

a. Ideally guess or identify the <u>original</u> trigger. Because the monkey hasn't yet been dealt with, it's likely that this problem has accumulated and repeated itself throughout your life, building up more and more tower blocks. Be careful not to take a midway event, such as when you were 20 years old. Really focus on the *original* one, the very first time when the monkey was born.

b. If you aren't getting an event from when you were really young, just ask your monkey this question.

TO TOPPLE THE TOWER WE NEED TO FIND THE VERY FIRST FOUNDATION BLOCK THAT WAS LAID. IF YOU /I WERE TO KNOW WHAT WAS THE VERY FIRST EVENT, THE FIRST EVENT THAT, WHEN UNCOVERED, WILL TOPPLE THE TOWER, WHAT WOULD THAT BE?

6. Repeat this exercise, writing the answers down for all of your main monkeys

7. Answer the questions as quickly as possible remembering the first answers that come to mind are normally the best ones. Some people will quickly be able to connect and empathise with their monkeys and others may take a little longer

If you need to take a break, please do so but here are a few monkey traps to avoid:

✗ Stopping halfway through dealing with a monkey. That's the monkey's self-defence mechanism. Don't fall for it. Only take a break in between monkeys!

✗ Make sure those mischievous monkeys don't throw you off track. Before going to a break always commit to a time and date that you're going to continue the process, even if it's just 10 minutes later!

✓ This exercise may take a few minutes or a few hours, but as you begin to connect with the monkeys you should start to feel as if the monkeys' disempowering beliefs are beginning to fall away or disappear, and at the very least begin to crack and crumble. I know it all sounds a little hard to believe but this process really works!

✓ If you don't have a buddy working with you, some people find it helpful to imagine inviting each monkey one by one into a shrink's office, asking them to lie on the couch and then asking them the specific questions

✓ Some people like to record the questions and play them back so they can answer off the cuff. However you find it easiest to get the answers, that's great, go ahead and do that now

✓ If you find yourself laughing with @(O_O)@ that's a good way both to pay them some attention and to get them in perspective at the same time. Not only is laughing fun, it also releases feel good chemicals called endorphins and those start to make us feel good about presenting

✓ Some of you may have struggled to raise a smile previously about the topic — but as you begin to change your outlook and approach, you'll notice how old fears and nerves are beginning to decrease and their grip loosen. Notice some of the monkeys are so absurd that you just have to smile or laugh with them!

Now you have a list of monkeys that you have connected with and you know where they came from and what they were trying to protect you from — the next stage is to grade @(O_O)@ using the traffic light system. This gives an opportunity to evaluate the status of your @(O_O)@ taming process.

Monkeys' Traffic Lights

The next step is that we need to separate out which monkeys we need to challenge next and which ones we need to put to the side for a moment. Monkey traffic lights use colours to grade the @(O_O)@. Green for go ahead and listen to these monkeys then pop them to one side. Amber for caution and Red for stop listening to their mutterings ASAP!

Green

The green monkeys are totally grounded and logical – the monkey's telling you something you know is totally true so you can go ahead and listen to the Green monkeys. e.g. *"You don't know how to use PowerPoint®"*. If you haven't used PowerPoint® before then what the monkey is saying is totally true. You don't yet know how to use PowerPoint®. You may however know how to use other software systems so just make sure these @(O_O)@ stay in perspective. We will revisit the Green monkeys concerns from Chapter 6 onwards where I share actual skills. With Green monkeys all that needs to be learnt is how to overcome that missing skill or knowledge gap, so you can park the Green monkeys for now.

Amber

The Amber monkey has some small point to share but is being a bit of a drama queen about it. It's likely he's exaggerating the issue and blowing it all out of proportion. The Amber monkey's trying to point things out that may have a small element of truth.

E.g. *"You're a rubbish presenter!"* Perhaps when you spoke in public before it didn't go so well, or perhaps you only **imagined** it didn't go well. The monkey might be saying that it could have gone better and maybe if you'd prepared or practised more it would have gone better. While that may be true and you want to take on board the learnings, it doesn't make you a "rubbish" presenter; that's all a bit over the top! Listen to the Amber monkey with caution.

Red

A Red monkey is one that's *totally* confused. It's just totally misunderstood some pieces of information. Or perhaps he hopes by exaggerating them and making them into a real drama you'll pay him some attention. You need to stop believing the Red monkeys ASAP.

For example a Red monkey would be, "You <u>can't</u> stand up in front of 20 people!"

Well you can – of course you can and you know it – so that's such an exaggeration. OK, so you may be a little apprehensive and you may need to learn some tips to calm yourself and get your breathing right, but fundamentally the monkey isn't telling the truth.

When I take my clients through this and we really interrogate the monkeys, the dramatic exaggerations and generalisations get uncovered and start unravelling right before their eyes!

A client of mine told me she had the "You can't stand up in front of 20 people" monkey, and when I started to dig a bit deeper it turns out she had in fact already given a reading in church in front of 100 people. OK, it wasn't a business setting, but notice how she could, and already has, stood up in front of five times more people than that and spoken. "How did the church event go?" I asked. "Well!" she said and started to smile!

"Monkey Tail"

One of the mums I worked with once uncovered at the root of her problem was that she hated "everyone looking at her". She found out that this arose from an incident in the school play when she "said something wrong" and felt that everyone was staring at her. The monkey was born and from then on told her to avoid speaking in public. As she got older, her @(O_O)@ applied that to other areas and that's when the problem really festered. She realised she had never learnt to "speak her mind".

The original event had been blown way out of proportion. It might be classed as a Red @(O_O)@ if it told her "You should never stand up in front of others". Once she realised the monkey was trying to protect her but was being a real drama queen, she decided to change her attitude, and therefore her monkey, to Amber — warning her to think before you speak —often helpful advice! Moving the monkey from Red to Amber was a significant achievement. She then used Golden rule#3 (coming soon) to turn it to a Green monkey; one appropriately balanced for the situation.

Exercise – Grading your monkey colour

1. With your buddy or on your own take each of your underneath monkeys and grade them allocating each a traffic light colour in your workbook. Green with a relevant point, Amber with a small point hidden away under all that exaggeration or Red, not to be listened to — he just got totally confused, is playing the drama queen or has generalized the situation way too much.

2. If you have any Red monkeys, look at them and notice they're drama queens, but also check and see if there's a reason you can't let them go yet. Perhaps you need to learn something about yourself or give yourself some credit before this @(O_O)@ will allow you to let it go completely.

3. If you have any Amber @(O_O)@ you know they're blown out of all proportion but that there *is* a tiny piece of learning the monkey wants you to learn from or be aware of. The @(O_O)@ holds a small element of truth about one area of presenting and, once you know about it, you'll be able to improve on that if you choose. It's OK to want to improve, and while knowing you want to improve you can still be OK with being who you are. If we all had to wait until we were a perfect presenter to be confident and like ourselves we might be waiting quite a long time! Be OK with making a few mistakes along the way.

4. Take the Amber and Red monkeys through to the next step – challenging the monkeys

5. Leave the Green monkeys to one side for the moment; they're just a case of a missing skill so you don't need to challenge them — just learn the skill or solve the problem in a different way! I'll cover the main skills you need in Chapters 6,7 & 8. Some people tell me they've tried to learn presentation skills before, but if the mischievous monkeys were in the way last time it would have been hard to really learn anything; your mind would have been too full of chatter. By the end of this process you'll have adopted much more helpful beliefs to aid your learning and personal development. With the monkeys on side it will be a faster, fun and more effective way for you to learn new things.

6. Now revisit *the* confidence scale we mentioned earlier. As you picture this scale, rate how you feel on a confidence scale of 1 – 10, where 1 =no confidence at all and terrified and 10 is very confident, relaxed and looking forward to the next presentation. Mark your score in your workbook and notice how things are already improving.

Some people have already got rid of a significant amount of their @(O_O)@ by this point in the programme and have automatically started to think how they can turn them from Red to Amber and then Green monkeys. Remember however many or few Red and Amber monkeys you have left, you must do the final exercise, "Challenging the Monkeys". Don't let the little fellas trick you out of completing the exercises fully!

3) How to Challenge your PUBLIC SPEAKING MONKEYS®

You're probably already realising now that you should NEVER take what the @(O_O)@ say at face value — they can be mischievous, as you already know. This final step of the three is to challenge the @(O_O)@. We need to end up with either no monkeys or only Green monkeys by the end of this chapter. As you know from the case study of Georgie's monkeys, the main aim of the technique is to see how out of date and old the monkeys' beliefs are and to learn from that in some way. Taking the monkeys to court dissolves the monkeys' disempowering beliefs through a series of specific questions designed to eat away at the unreal and outdated beliefs.

Before you start, it's helpful to know a little more about how the monkeys come about and what they think their purpose is.

Monkeys take things literally

When we're younger we tend to think that the adults and especially those in positions of authority are always right. We believe that the words they say are literal and 100% true, because they often are. If a teacher says 2+2 =4 then we automatically believe them. We don't question it, so our brains are then wired to do the same with everything that person says, no matter what. If the teacher tells you "That's a silly answer" you'll automatically believe that to be the absolute truth.

Your answer probably wasn't a "silly" answer; I mean what *is* a silly answer anyway? How would you know if you came across one? Most answers are either the one that's expected from the teacher or a different one.

Let's play this out: If you put forward a different answer it's likely to have been based on:

> ➤ Things you may have heard other people say. Perhaps you were just repeating what you'd heard previously. That's not a silly answer then, is it? It may not be right but it isn't "silly"

> ➤ Thinking laterally — thinking of things that in your mind were related. Either seeing the question in a different way or the answer. Just because you were thinking about the question in a different way doesn't mean it was "silly"

> ➤ You might have been playing the class fool and trying to be silly on purpose. If you gave a "silly" answer on purpose, but one that is related, then that's the basis of all good jokes. Perhaps you're really a comedian.

> ➤ If you have feelings of worry around making a mistake, and if it was this specific event that comes to mind, it's likely that you actually wanted to give the right answer. Maybe you didn't understand the question; maybe the teacher didn't phrase it as clearly as they might.

> ➤ Maybe you didn't know the answer — in which case you just tried your best and you could argue that the teacher hadn't taught you in a manner that you could understand!

There are many more options and the point is that it probably wasn't true; you didn't give a "silly" answer.

Monkeys take things out of proportion

When we're young, we have such a small set of people around us with whom we spend bucket loads of time it means that any one of them saying something less than positive might have a real impact on our young minds. Monkeys always take things personally, which means that feedback, for example, can be blown way out of proportion.

Another less obvious bad habit that can occur is making negative generalisations from one single thing in the past. In their haste to protect you, the monkeys can apply a single learning to all sorts of other areas of your life. For example, the "You can't read " @(O_O)@ may have decided that volunteering to speak in any school lesson on any subject was too high a risk. As you get older @(O_O)@ might then think it's helpful to apply that learning to other areas such as team meetings, PTAs and appraisals. That's when the problem really festers – and you never learn to voice your opinion. Anything the monkey sees as similar or the same circumstances can be affected — and clearly, in this example, it's way out of proportion with the original trigger.

"Monkey Tail"

Someone who attended one of my workshops drilled down to their underneath monkey and told us they remembered their dad had said "You're rubbish". It was clearly a significantly emotional monkey for them but at an initial glance this may seem a fairly common or low grade turn of phrase. But think for a moment what it means if you believe it to be literally true.

What happens to the rubbish every week or so? Yes, it gets thrown away, put outside and left for some strangers to come and take away in their truck. We uncovered the learning – they saw they had taken it too literally and it was just something their dad said mindlessly when they were young to try and help them improve and get better (even though it may not have had the effect). Dad had only said it because he loved them and wanted them to succeed.

Immediately once uncovered, that monkey just released its hold on the person.

Monkeys stay stuck in the mud

It is important to thank the monkeys for their role in your life because the approach they used may have been very appropriate at the time of the first incident. Helping us to avoid situations where people laugh at us, for example. Perhaps when growing up this may have been the very best way to deal with the problem (Remember when the monkeys and you were young we didn't have the experience and knowledge we have today — we had fewer options and solutions available to us than we do now as adults). Now we know plenty of ways to deal with different situations if they arise, but at the time, at only five for example, we perhaps only had a few choices.

The problem is that we stick to our guns and unintentionally stay forever with that one limiting decision or "bad" choice we made. Unless we re-evaluate and refresh our thoughts through this process we're stuck with them — whether they work for us or not. So now's the time to deal with it in another way – see the original event for what it was, use it as positive learning and approach it with as positive an attitude as possible. Often the event is tiny, and realising that it's there makes it disappear.

Now you know that the monkeys have some fatal flaws it's time to go back and free yourself from their grasp. As you work through your monkeys, notice these traits I've mentioned and help your monkeys fly the nest or grow up into helpful monkeys living in the real world and not stuck in the past.

Exercise — Challenging your monkeys

"Taking the monkeys to court"

This approach questions the very basis of the negative and unhelpful beliefs your monkey have, to get right to the heart of the disempowering beliefs and thoughts and systematically, one by one, blow each negative belief to pieces!

Exercise – Challenging the monkeys — Take monkey to court

This technique uses a series of specifically designed questions to get to the heart of the monkey and blow apart his fibbing stories. For this to work, you must answer the question directly as if you were in the dock of a courtroom. You cannot waffle around the answer! All the time, the questions themselves work at a specific level to break down any false logic in the monkey's argument.

> **All the time, the questions themselves work at a specific level to break down any false logic in the monkey's argument.**

Even though I set these very clear instructions, there are always the odd few people who decide to do this in their own way. If it works that's fine, but often it doesn't. Just follow the instructions – don't let the monkeys take you off track, and see that this is the final step in taming those monkeys!

1. Remember, we're getting rid of negative Red & Amber monkeys, so if a statement is positive you won't want to ask these questions. Remind yourself of Georgie's case study quickly before doing this exercise "live"

2. NEVER skim through the questions quickly. ALWAYS take one question at a time and let it sink deep into your mind

3. Watch out! Stubborn monkeys might try to set their monkey traps to try and throw you off track. They might also tempt you not to take the questions in because they may sense that their habitat and way of life is under threat because you want to change. Monkeys don't like that much!

4. Work through any remaining Amber monkeys. Get the hang of the process and get a taste for the questions detailed below. Finish with the Red @(O_O)@. Keep going until each monkey's either disappeared or have turned into Green @(O_O)@ with a real and logical problem you know it's possible to find a solution for

5. Depending on how good you are at communicating with your @(O_O)@, how mischievous they're feeling and how effectively you completed the previous chapter's exercises, the "taking the monkeys to court" exercise might last anything from 10 minutes to several hours

6. If you have lots of stubborn @(O_O)@ you'll need to take a break. The important thing is to have been successful at getting rid of, or significantly downgrading, at least three of them before you take a break. Then you know you can do it. Take a break if you need to and come back to it. DONT be tempted to leave it till tomorrow. DO complete this process in one go

7. Ask each monkey the following questions (the majority will be relevant and a few less so) and log your answers in your workbook:

    a. HOW DO YOU <u>KNOW</u> THAT THE MONKEY'S TELLING THE TRUTH?

    b. IF YOU TOOK IT TO COURT, WOULD THE MONKEY HAVE ANY <u>EVIDENCE</u> AGAINST YOU?

    c. IN COURT, WHAT EVIDENCE DO YOU HAVE TO THE CONTRARY? WHAT WOULD BE YOUR DEFENCE?

    d. IN WHAT WAY IS THIS MONKEY BEING RIDICULOUS?

    e. WOULD YOU SAY THESE THINGS TO YOUR BEST FRIEND?

    f. HAVE YOU CONSIDERED THAT IN ORDER TO BE PERFECT, YOU NEED IMPERFECTIONS?

    g. IF YOU HAVE HAD SOME NEGATIVE FEEDBACK IN THE PAST:

        i. HOW MANY PEOPLE SAID THAT SPECIFIC THING TO YOU?

      ii. HOW MANY PEOPLE HAVE NEVER MENTIONED THAT SPECIFIC THING?

      iii. HAS ANYONE SAID THAT IT WENT WELL?

      iv. WHY DIDN'T YOU BELIEVE THEM? DO THEY OFTEN LIE?

  h. THINK ABOUT THE LANGUAGE THE MONKEY USES — IF THEY USE THE WORD "NEVER", E.G. "I NEVER LIKE SPEAKING IN PUBLIC" ASK:

      i. WHAT DO YOU MEAN, NEVER?

      ii. WHAT, NEVER EVER?

      iii. HAS THERE EVER BEEN A TIME WHEN YOU DID?

  i. IF THEY USE THE WORD "ALWAYS", E.G. "I ALWAYS FORGET WHAT TO SAY", ASK:

      i. WHAT, ALWAYS?

      ii. EVERY SINGLE TIME?

      iii. HAS THERE EVER BEEN A TIME WHEN YOU DIDN'T?

  j. IF THEY USE THE WORD "CAN'T", ASK:

      i. WHAT DO YOU MEAN, CAN'T?

      ii. DO YOU MEAN YOU HAVEN'T YET?

      iii. OR THAT YOU DID ALREADY, EVEN IF IT WASN'T PERFECT FIRST TIME ROUND?

8. Use all of the specifically designed questions to help you to overcome the monkey battle in your head. They aren't the only questions that can be used but they are specifically scripted ones that will go to the heart of a monkey to stop any fighting. One or two may not make sense for your specific monkey, but most of the questions should

9. You might need to change the questions very slightly depending on whether your monkey is phrased positively or negatively. Most monkeys are phrased negatively. e.g. "You're rubbish" so the questions are designed accordingly. If you need to adapt them slightly then make the questions work for your monkey.

10. Use your confidence charm whenever you need to — just press your left thumb and middle finger together

Monkey buddy instructions & warnings

- As a monkey buddy you're an unbiased bystander and should be able to see or guess which questions make sense and which ones genuinely don't. Most or all of the questions will be relevant — it's only one or two that may not and which your buddy won't be able to answer. Use your intuition to see if your partner's answering truthfully. The way to do this is to run them through your mind. Imagine you had the monkey they're working on at that moment and ask yourself that question about that monkey

- Indicators that you're asking a relevant question for that monkey:

  o You deliver the question and your partner becomes quiet and seems to be focusing on the inside. Their eyes might roam in different directions as if they're searching for the right answer. They then answer you and begin to see how their answers aren't really based on fact. Let them work through this themselves. You might not need to say a word other than encouraging "Mmms" and nods

  o Your partner might not actually even need to verbalise the answer to the question out loud. They may just have a realisation inside their head and then say, "Yeah, OK". You know that this has happened because there'll be a shift in their body language and facial expressions — remember to use your intuition to see that your partner's genuinely got rid of the problem. If the answer isn't confidential it's best to verbally check with them they've got rid of the monkey simply by asking them, "What did you learn from that?

o   Your partner gets agitated and defensive, stroppy or distracts you. Here's a list of things I've seen, all with the sole purpose of avoiding the question:

✗   They try to "attack" you (only verbally!) in order to avoid answering the question e.g. "Well you aren't any good at speaking in public! I don't know why I'm asking you to help!"

✗   They claim they'll leave this for a better time. Trust me there won't be a "better time" and anyway they were the ones that asked you to do this now

✗   They give you a rational and logical reason why they should skip that question e.g. "Well that might take me some time to think about so let's skip that one and I'll come back to it tomorrow". Trust me, "tomorrow" will never come

•   If the question genuinely isn't needed, your partner won't get annoyed or frustrated with you asking it the once – they'll just say in a normal tone, "I don't think that's relevant". If they start to get agitated and you only asked once so far, it's highly likely there's a monkey there! Thank you for putting your friend's best interest first

•   If your partner's finding it less easy to get in touch with the "challenge the monkey" questions you might need to take a little bit longer to help them. If your partner starts to protest, remind them of the goal they asked you to come and help overcome: this @(O_O)@. Remind them that the ultimate goal is worth going through some bumps along the way for

Go ahead and challenge the monkeys – keep going until all of them are done!

Now you have tamed your monkeys

Well done on completing the Challenging the Monkeys section – you've overcome a massive hurdle that was in the way of your success – excellent. What I'm looking for in your progress at this point is not that you're necessarily immediately ready to deliver a fantastic presentation, but that you've tamed those exaggerating and confusing monkeys; that now you have what others would say is a "reasonable mindset" for the task in hand. If your presentation's the first you've ever done to 20 people and it's tomorrow, you may have a few jitters and that's those hormones running around your body. I'll give you the tools in the next chapter so you know how to manage that. It's OK if there are some gaps in your knowledge because there are a few things you need to learn to help you along the way. You'll need some tips and techniques to satisfy those Green monkeys so they can stop worrying about you.

The aim of challenging the monkeys is solely to get those unhelpful monkey beliefs back into perspective. Get them all to become Green monkeys who want to help you or disappear completely if they have nothing to help you with. The final step is to also be OK now with the small possibility that some of these things might actually happen — so you need to learn the skills or attitudes to deal with them. That's what the next chapter is about – learning the skills and attitudes to deal with any of the challenges if they do occur.

Now the @(O_O)@ know you're paying them attention. As each one brings you an issue you can deal with them one by one. Instead of their screaming all together so none of them can be heard, you're clearing the airwaves for the relevant messages to get through more clearly. It's a bit like radio interference; the Red and Amber @(O_O)@ were making the line so crackly that you couldn't hear the important underlying message.

Of course, you haven't test driven your new skills yet so you may not know for sure that the monkeys have totally disappeared, but you're relying on that feeling inside that they have gone.

Remember, the skills chapter has to come after the taming the monkeys process because you'll only take on board the tips fully AFTER your monkeys are tamed or have gone away. There's no point learning a skill if your beliefs and monkeys don't support you or want you to learn — they'll just sabotage your brave attempts. Now the monkeys are on side you'll find it easy to learn and practise these techniques. Those might be new techniques or ones you'd heard of before but just not implemented. Now is the time!

Now would be a great time to revisit your confidence scale and see how your confidence has significantly increased. The scale is from 1 – 10 where 1 =no confidence at all and terrified and 10 is very confident, relaxed and looking forward to the next presentation.

I'm not promising that you'll never have another monkey again, because that's not realistic. It's good to have monkeys, and as soon as you start stretching yourself and going outside of your comfort zone you'll come across new monkeys; perhaps ones you don't even know exist yet. The trick is to have the power, knowledge and experience of dealing with the monkeys. Once you've done it once and continue to practise it more and more you'll know that there's no situation for which you won't have the tools to tame the monkeys involved.

Key takeaways

✓ There are three golden rules in the taming the monkeys process

    o   Golden Rule # 1: Catch Your Monkeys

    o   Golden Rule # 2: Connect With Your Monkeys

    o   Golden Rule # 3: Challenge Your Monkeys

✓ Before going ahead and catching your monkeys for real, you familiarised yourself with the chapter- the teachings and exercise preparation. This meant that your motivation for getting through was clear in your mind and all the previous exercises leading up to this point had been completed effectively. Also you were ready to complete the taming process in one swoop to avoid monkey distractions!

✓ You then created a confidence charm to use at any point throughout the taming process.

✓ When you completed the catching your monkeys exercise you realised the importance of catching all of them, no matter how small, large or silly.

✓ Then to ensure you had identified the underneath monkey you reviewed the monkeys to check they were Specific, Separate, Small and Simple following the 4S Monkey checklist

✓ Next was connecting – we got to understand the monkeys a little more, and how:

    o   Monkeys have your "best interests at heart" and (over) protect you

    o   Each monkey has a personal life purpose e.g. to stop you repeating a "mistake"

    o   Each monkey has its unique date of birth when a trigger event happened

    o   Monkeys are out of date because they haven't been updated

    o   Monkeys are over sensitive – they always take things too personally o   Monkeys love to be drama queens — they love to blow things out of proportion

✓   To connect with your monkeys you uncovered each event that caused the monkeys to arise

o   Monkey by monkey we identified the event

o   The monkeys were then graded using the traffic light system

✓   The final part involved challenging the monkeys where you took the monkeys to court

o   By challenging you monkeys you were able to neutralise them

o   The questions broke down the false logic in the monkey's argument

✓   We learnt a little more about monkey tendencies like

o   Monkeys take things literally

o   Monkeys take things out of proportion

o   Monkeys stay stuck in the mud

Of course you haven't test driven your new skills yet so you may not know for sure that the monkeys have totally disappeared, but you're relying on that feeling inside that they have gone.

Well done. Now you have tamed your monkeys, move on to the next chapter so you can go ahead and train those monkeys into new and helpful behaviours, including how to be OK with not being perfect all the time. Move on to the next chapter from here because the rest of this chapter is only for those few people who may not have yet followed the instructions perfectly, may have fallen for a monkey trick or have some other reason for not taming all of their monkeys yet. see you in Chapter 6!

In the rare event all your monkeys aren't tamed yet

It's OK if you feel you haven't tamed all your monkeys yet. Like anything, this is a learning process, and in order to get the right result, all of the steps need to be followed. It's highly likely that without realising it you've fallen for one of those pesky monkeys' traps!

Remember, there's no failure, only feedback. So the feedback is that something hasn't had the desired response in the taming process for you yet. If none of your monkeys have gone and you feel no different, you've either fallen for a monkey trick along the way or not completed the exercises completely.

Never mind, I've created a checklist for such an occasion:

1. Have you answered the questions in Chapter 1? Did you have a really compelling reason for starting this "Taming the Monkeys" process?

    a. Do you have a true feel for how much discomfort the monkeys are causing you

    b. Do you appreciate how much more you will have when they are gone?

2. Are you doing it for your own reasons? Some people are just doing the process because they were told to or someone suggested it to them, but

if you haven't got in touch with your own personal reasons for doing it the process is less likely to work for you

3. A common mistake is for people to want to remain in total control during the exercises; not to relax into them and let go of the need to be right. Just relax and answer the questions in this programme from the top of your mind or your gut feel, not the logical and calculating part of your brain.

4. Is there some element of a "positive side effect" to keeping your monkey that you are worried about letting go of? If that's the case you need to find & separate out the positive element. Then develop another way of achieving that positive so you can then let go of the monkey. For example if "You're not good enough" monkey has made the person a high achiever – they will need to decide how to motivate themselves in another way before letting go of the monkey. For example they could decide they will now motivate themselves towards aiming for what they do want – e.g. How great it will fee to achieve X.

5. Did you read through and take on board the thoughts and ideas presented in Chapter 3 or did you just skip through them? Taking on board the elements involved in gaining successful change is a key learning for life — not just monkey taming — so it's well worth reading through and spending the time on:

    a. Motivation – the energy to want to learn the new thing

    b. Belief– that you can learn it so you begin the learning process

    c. Skills – you need to know how to learn the new thing

    d. Action – a change of behaviour to begin and practise new skills

    e. Feedback – doing the new thing for real and then getting feedback

6. Did you read through the Chapter 4 case study and get inside the mind of Georgie? Could you empathise with her monkeys and see where they came from and how she tamed them? Often, seeing how others deal with their challenges is easier than doing it yourself, which is why I included that chapter prior to you taming your own monkeys — so you could learn and experience the process before going ahead and taming the monkeys yourself

7. Have you been writing all your answers down in in your workbook? As previously mentioned, physically writing the answer has multiple benefits including making answers appear more real: it makes you acknowledge the presence of monkeys or limiting beliefs and then there is nowhere to hide! If you have been writing everything down, well done. It will make it easier for you to track where in the process any problem is arising. Review your notes and see if during any specific exercises you feel you could do even better.

8. Did you recruit a monkey buddy? Even if you haven't worked with a buddy up until now, if you have a few stubborn monkeys left it's strongly recommended that you find yourself a buddy or a good friend to do this last bit with

   a. They don't need to answer the questions themselves; they can just help you to do it. You could show them the monkey buddy letter in Chapter 4 to help them get up to speed with where you are now

   b. Having someone who'll hold you accountable to answering the questions is priceless

9. Did you find the "underneath" monkeys for ALL of your monkeys and did they ALL pass the 4S checklist or did you skip a few, maybe because you thought they were similar?

   a. To be effective you must have broken the problem down into small, specific, simple and separate monkeys.

   b. For example, the "I can't use the flip chart" monkey might drill down into the "You can't spell" and "No one can read your handwriting" monkeys. Each one of those will need to be challenged separately because, as you can see, they're totally different problems. Trying to tackle them together would be too confusing

10. Did you connect to the original event and get a rough age? Was it before you were 7 or so years old?

    a. If the event you connected to was at an older age, such as 20, it might be that you haven't connected with the first time it happened. That was just another example of it happening later in life. 20 may be the first time but it's very unlikely

    b. Spend a little more time focusing on getting in touch with that first event or trigger that caused the monkey to be born

c. Remember you can quickly move on to the next step. You only need to spend a few seconds there as long as you connect. Remember "guessing" is OK

11. Confidence charm – do you feel safe and OK doing the process knowing you have the confidence charm or some other positive thoughts to help you over any bumps? Perhaps you need to be sure you have the positive place you can go to help you move onto the upward spiral whenever you need to. Use the confidence charm or a picture you love or a teddy bear! Whatever helps you feel good, confident happy and safe.

12. Have you excused yourself from a challenge question or two for no reason? Occasionally the @(O_O)@ are so clever that they trick you into believing those questions aren't relevant to you — so you skip over all the questions saying "That's not the right question for me!". Go back and check you have a genuine reason if you have skipped any of the questions – the only valid reason being that the question isn't relevant to my monkey, not "I find it difficult to answer that question"!

13. Do you suffer from perfectionism? Some clients feel that they have to be perfect and I talk about this in the next chapter under "mindset". If this is you, read the next section on mindset only and then either your fears will have gone or you'll be in the right place to go through the process again and this time make it work for you. I've seen perfectionism have a few effects on the taming process:

a. Inaction – the person has not started any process of DOING the exercises. They've read them but not started because the fear of not being right or perfect prevents them from starting. Go ahead and read the next section, then begin the process

b. Unconvinced – the client has tamed all their monkeys perfectly well to my satisfaction but because they aren't sure they did everything perfectly they aren't perfectly sure they've tamed their monkeys! Read the next section and see that you've already tamed your monkeys. Stop wasting time – just move forward and learn how to train them

14. Are you OK with it being quick and easy? Many of my clients can't believe how quickly this process works, because they've had their fears for so long. But that's like me saying to a computer repairman, "I don't believe you can remove this computer virus in just in a few hours because it's been there for years!" The length of

time taken to get @(O_O)@ under control is NOT proportional to the size of the monkey or how long you've had them! Some clients used to think that they needed to take ages getting rid of them because they had had them for so long! Well you can if you want to, but why not just move on to training the fellas?

15. Some people just have invisible monkeys. No matter how hard you look or how well you do the process the money is invisible to you. It's a bit like when you find it easy to see what other people need to do, but not so easy for yourself. If that's the case, you'll need a professional money tamer to help – only they will be able to see it and show it to you. Take a look at my website www.DeeClayton.com and the training and coaching options there to find one that suits you. You might want to work with me one to one through personal coaching or in bite size chunks with the interactive Fear Free Home learning programme. Take a look at the website as there is something there for everyone and every budget or just email me for more information dee@deeclayton.com.

Now that you've identified the problem and tamed your personal monkeys it's the right time to learn some new skills. I'll introduce you to the most helpful attitudes to have from a mindset point of view. After all, until now, your mind had been full of negative monkey chatter and now there's space to introduce some more helpful positive monkey attitudes so you can continue on the upward spiral of speaking success. Your body language is also vital to a healthy mindset so I'll cover that too, showing you how to remain calm, relaxed and ready for anything just by the way you stand!

Training your monkeys

Welcome to the next part of this book, where we begin the process of training the monkeys; where you'll learn how to ask them to work with you so that you can be a good speaker. I share a huge selection of tips and tricks that have worked for my clients for many years and these new approaches and techniques can only be learnt, absorbed and used after the monkeys have been tamed. This is by no means the only training you can do but my aim is for it to be an excellent start. Even if you only implemented one or two of these ideas, let alone all of them, your speaking skills would dramatically improve.

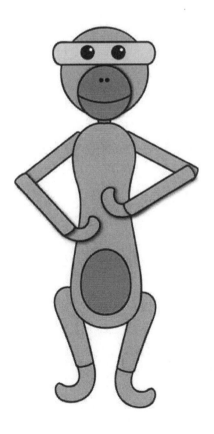

Chapter 6 -
Mindset and body language

The content for this next chapter is pulled together by answering some of the most common questions from mentoring clients. By this point, as they start to ask these questions, I'm delighted - it means no more monkeys getting in the way; they just want to get on and become a good speaker.

Obviously there's more depth to each and every technique – but in the interest of keeping this book from becoming an encyclopaedia I thought I'd just summarize them so you can begin to practise the ideas yourself.

I could talk for hours on this topic – in fact I often do in training courses. But this isn't the book for that. This book's about taming the monkeys - and now they're tamed you might have a few Green ones left that are genuine and telling the truth. Because you may have avoided speaking for so long it's very likely that you have a few questions or missing skills. You've been so busy before worrying about your monkeys you probably didn't get much of a chance to focus on:

A. Your mindset & body language

B. Preparation - structure and content

C. Practice

D. Stand and deliver

E. Feedback

Each of these is important, and your mindset is the most important, which is why you needed to clear away the less positive monkeys to make room for new, helpful thoughts. Your body language will mostly come from your mindset, so now you're feeling more positive your body language will express that too. However you may need to unlearn some bad habits, so let's take a look at what to do instead of that old behaviour.

Have you ever had the experience when someone wanted to say something to you but the way they said it made you feel bad? Then a nicer friend with a more gentle way comes to tell you the same thing but manages to say it in a way that actually felt good – how did they do that? They may have said the same thing but in different language. That's what we're going to teach our monkeys to do - tell us their message in a more positive way; to be constructive and not destructive.

Let go of thinking you have to be perfect

Many people might call it perfectionism, or a need for everything to be "just so" or exactly the way they want it. Some people may not want to start something unless they know it will be perfect. If they start, perhaps they worry whether they're doing it right. But ironically they're less likely to be doing it right because they aren't focusing on the task; they're focusing on the worry! Of course this is a kind of monkey; this belief may be impacting on many other areas of life too, not just presenting. It can bring troubles and challenges even if you did know what "perfect" or "just so" looked like anyway.

As we start to listen to and connect with this monkey, many of my clients start telling me how it's the same in their home or work life. They need everything to be tidy: their desk, car or homes. But not just tidy, it needs to be "perfect", which can be less than easy for others sharing the space with them —workmates or family etc. (Let me tell you, I know because I used to live with one before I learnt all about this stuff!). Things become easier if you can put this to one side for this process. Just tame that monkey too if you choose to. Here are a few thoughts for you to consider with the aim of unpicking the perfectionism monkey's impossible standards.

Nobody's perfect

In order that you can challenge the perfection monkey you need to first realise why it causes problems. Have you heard of the phrase "nobody's perfect?" Think about it. No one's perfect, are they? The reason perfection is an issue is because nobody else in the world is perfect - yet you've set yourself an impossibly high bar to reach: of perfection. That hardly seems fair. Get my drift?

Imperfections are what make us human.. Imperfections apparently are the basis of evolution so imperfections make us perfect as we are. I believe you are perfect only when you realise it's OK that you aren't.

Let me ask you this: Who do you know that's perfect? If some people's names have come to mind, consider whether they're really perfect or whether they have imperfections and weaknesses.

> **Imperfections are what make us human. Imperfections apparently are the basis of evolution so imperfections make us perfect as we are. I believe you are perfect only when you realise it's OK that you aren't.**

Everybody has weaknesses of some kind. They might be excellent in one area; they may be a genius on another topic - but it doesn't mean they're perfect. I'd think that if you look at other areas of their life they probably don't have 100% success. Look at their family life. Is that perfect? Look at their financial life. Is that perfect? Look at their fitness. Is that perfect? Do they know the answers to every question? If you look hard enough, you'll find plenty of areas where that person's not perfect.

Of course you can still admire people, respect people and learn from them but they don't have to be perfect for you to admire them and learn from them. I suppose a good idea would be to pick different people with different strengths in distinct areas and "model" or copy the best behaviours of each. (These are actually the origins of NLP).

Some of the people some of the time

It is very difficult to prove that you're acting or behaving in a perfect manner unless you know what perfection looks like. So my questions to you are "What does perfection look like?" and "How would you know if you were perfect?". The answers many clients give me to this question are "I wouldn't be doing anything wrong and everyone would like me". It's very hard, if not impossible, never to do anything wrong in anyone's eyes. I'm sure you've heard the phrase, "You can please some of the people some of the time but you can't please all of the people all of the time".

"Monkey Tail"

I once sat in a very "salesy" seminar - you may know the kind of tactics I mean by "salesy". Long sales letters with thousands of testimonials, yellow highlighting in the text and handwritten script clearly digitally printed with the 10 reasons why my life wouldn't be right unless I turned up to the seminar. There were 150 people present and the man at the front of the room was well aware that his style was offensive to many. He asked bold as brass, "How many of you don't like me?".

After getting over the "un-Britishness" of the question, about half the room put up their hands.

"Wow, how brave of him!" I thought (and I was one of the ones with my hand up).

Then he said a very powerful thing:

"Yes, but you're still here aren't you!"

Mmm, good point!

Whatever you do, even if millions of people think you're fantastic and what you're doing's exactly right, there'll always be some people who don't believe that everything you do is perfect. If you're going to put yourself out there and speak in public you have to be prepared for people not to always agree with everything you say. In fact some people even encourage healthy debate to fuel word of mouth! Think about most news interviews – they have someone "for" the argument and someone "against" the argument to make sure it's interesting and balanced, but also entertaining.

There are going to be other presentation skills trainers, voice trainers, psychologists, NLPers etc, reading this book, but I can't please them all. To think that I could is unrealistic and would just cause me so much stress and worry that I'd never write another word. It's also totally possible that as you read this you won't completely agree with everything I say. You may not fully buy into every single idea in here. But as long as you associate with enough of it that you follow the exercises and get a great result for yourself, my job is done... As long as you reach more of your potential than you had before, I'm happy.

When I'm speaking I don't want half the room to dislike me, but I've got over my monkey that *everyone* has to love me. The way you know you're on track and have a message worth saying is that some people will agree with what you're saying and start to "follow" you (hopefully not literally down the street) and some people will also start to disagree, or say the opposite. Take that as a good sign; almost all of the world's best speakers and change agents attract people who have different points of views and often "upset" a few people on the way. They're brave enough and bold enough and confident enough in their own message, get on their soap box and stand up to be heard. Whether you want to change the world, change the client's viewpoint or get the audience to think in a different way, you have to be OK with not all of them liking or loving you immediately. Perhaps they won't like your message for a short time while they buy into it, perhaps it will be a few days, weeks or years till they realise you were right. Perhaps they'll never agree with your view. Be OK with that, accept it and then, just by embracing it, ironically you'll be reducing the number of times it happens!

Let go of needing to be right all the time

If you have to be perfect or right all the time what would that look like? Would that mean that every single thing you did was absolutely correct? How would you know that everything you did was correct? The answer might be easier if you were doing a mathematical equation; they often have either correct or incorrect answers, but life in general –relationships, problems or challenges –

doesn't have black and white answers. There isn't always a right or wrong. There are often only *different* answers. Some of those might produce better results than others.

But have you ever noticed that until you commit to going down one road or following one decision you're never sure what the result or outcome is. What you might have thought was a perfect decision could turn out to have some external event impact, that you could never have predicted and which results in a less than perfect outcome. In areas that aren't black and white you'll never know whether your decision was perfect or not - you can only make the best decision on the information and feelings you had at the time.

> ### *"Imperfect action is better than perfect inaction."*
>
> ~Harry Truman

Maybe you've experienced this too – that when you wait until you know what the perfect outcome is, the perfect option you thought you'd take has disappeared. Imagine looking to buy a house and you see one that you really like but you continue to do more research until you're a hundred percent sure that this is the right one. You call the estate agent to put in an offer but you've already missed the boat. The house was sold to someone else while you were taking your time making a *"perfect"* decision. Of course you should do due diligence; what I'm proposing is that you only spend a "reasonable" amount of time fact-finding and deciding because otherwise the options might no longer be there. Which means you can't take a perfect decision anyway. In fact your decision was not perfect at all because it didn't end up with the result that you wanted. Perhaps you're beginning to see how this idea that everything must be perfect is not particularly helpful.

But how can I achieve without the perfection monkey?

Some clients believe that the perfection monkey is how they've progressed and moved forward in their life so far - and to some extent that may be true. Perhaps the monkey's driven you to more success than you'd have achieved without it. Perhaps the perfectionist monkey's enabled you to become top of your game - and that's excellent because once you get the monkey on your side he can still help you excel or, if you prefer, you can choose to do something else with your time. Perhaps you'll start working to the 80:20 rule with your time, using the theory that 80% of the results will come from a focus on only 20% of the projects or tasks. By identifying the right levers to pull, you'll be reducing your need to make everything perfect. Perhaps the extra hour you spend on adjusting the font size on your presentation isn't worth the hour that you aren't spending with your children or sleeping the night before the presentation. Perhaps you'll decide to do something differently or you may not. The benefit of connecting with and challenging your perfectionist monkey is that you can have choice. You can choose to be a perfectionist in some areas or you can choose not to be.

Perfect presentations

It is impossible to give a perfect presentation because you'd never know what perfect is. You can feel that you've done your best; you can feel that you've communicated all of the information in an effective manner. People might even come up to you and tell you what a brilliant presentation that was. But how would you know if it was "perfect"? We're back to the problem that perfection is impossible to define and measure - so why seek it?

In a presentation, set yourself a more measurable and realistic goal, for example that you "feel you did the best you could" or that "X% of the audience took the action you asked them to" or "the feedback gave an average score of Y out of 10". Remember that 10 out of 10 is a very tricky bar to reach with a group of people. I think there's only a certain type of person who gives 10 out of 10. If you speak to people who give a nine out of 10 and ask them what could have been done better in order to get a 10 out of 10 many of them say, "Nothing - but I never give 10 out of 10".

> **...perfection is impossible to define and measure - so why seek it?**

Our thoughts affect our body language

You may not fully believe this yet, so try this exercise below.

Look down to the floor and slump your shoulders, then try to think of something really positive, without changing your body position. You may just be able to *think* about something positive, but can you actually FEEL happy? Probably not.

Now look up to the ceiling, put a smile on your face, and try in vain to feel something just a little sad without changing your body language. It's difficult, right?

Mostly with the latter body language you can't help but feel positive, especially when you have a smile on your face. But what's that got to do with public speaking? No, I don't think you need to go on stage grinning like crazy. But do be aware that **our thinking does affect our body language.**

Even if you think your body language isn't showing, trust me, it will be. So you need to have your monkeys saying the right things in your head - and naturally better body language will follow. Equally if you have better body language it's easier to gain that feeling of confidence - so you'll want to learn how to have the optimal body language before even starting a presentation.

Calm and confident body language

People often ask how they should stand and what they should do with their arms. After taming the monkeys, the very next thing we do on our courses is to teach people the "Presenter or Trainer State", something I've adapted from David Shephard and Tad James' book *Presenting Magically*.

When we enter a stressful situation our "sympathetic nervous system" becomes active just for this kind of occasion and prepares our body for the challenge ahead. It gets our muscles ready for action, makes our heart beat faster; it makes our lungs work harder and sometimes gives us tunnel vision and all sorts of other helpful physical responses to a threat. Those are all life-saving responses if we were facing a physical danger, so it's good to have them. However, when it comes to public speaking it's less than helpful to have those reactions because they prevent us from thinking clearly. In fact, they're the ideal habitat for the untamed monkeys to have lots of fun in. So instead, you'll want to learn how to be calm and confident. Here's my summary of how to teach yourself the "presenter state" - a state or feeling in which you're totally calm, confident and grounded, ready for anything that comes your way. Once you've learnt it, you need to practise it and soon it will come naturally – you'll be presenting calmly and confidently without even noticing you're in "presenter state".

"I did my presentation yesterday - the one I was preparing for and it went really well. I used the Presenter State and didn't feel nervous at all. Your ideas have really worked. Thank you so much for all your help."

Danielle Fagot,
Independent Financial Adviser, RICHMOND HOUSE FINANCIAL SERVICES

Exercise – Presenter state

1. Take a few moments to clear all other thoughts from your mind - think only about the presentation and your audience

2. Get into "presenter ready" stance where your feet are parallel and a comfortable width apart and facing forwards. Your arms are nice and relaxed by your side and your back, neck and head are straight so you're standing tall. I notice people who do yoga, horse riding and other hobbies where posture is important are very good at standing up straight. Others who live and work on computers perhaps have a tendency to be slightly more hunched or rounded so may need to work a little harder. Ask your presentation buddy to look at your stance and straighten you up until you look more confident, taller and credible – all with the right stance

To get presenter stance correct it's often helpful to visualise your body as a set of tin cans stacked up on one another with two tin cans for each leg and a bigger tin can for the body with the arm cans resting quietly by the side. Any movement of the cans into a less even stance would make the tin tower unstable, which means your body's using up energy just to keep itself standing. Ideally, you want to benefit from an energy-neutral and grounded stance so that your energy can be used elsewhere and for other tasks

Become totally grounded. You may have heard of the term "being grounded" but plenty of people don't actually know how to "be grounded". I only became fully aware of the importance of this step when I had the pleasure of seeing Olive

Hickmott's work in action (a specialist in helping others to improve their health and learning). Being grounded is a feeling of being totally connected to the earth. It is the opposite of being light-headed because it focuses your energy in the feet. It may sound a little "hippie" but as always I'll just ask that you go along with me! As you're standing, imagine a connection with the earth so strong through your feet that you couldn't be blown or pushed off track even if anyone tried. You're firmly, comfortably and solidly attached to the floor. Some people imagine their favourite plants offering their support by holding onto their feet and using all their deep root system to keep you in strong contact with the earth

Control your breathing. This will make a huge difference. Take a few deep breaths in through your mouth and out through your nose and then carry on breathing normally. If you're wearing a microphone, do it quietly! If you start to speed up, take a deep breath, then a normal breath and continue. You can disguise this if you want by doing it while popping over to get a drink of water for example

3. Concentrate on one spot just behind the audience and slightly above their heads. By keeping your eyes on one single point of focus you can simultaneously and paradoxically see everything that is going on around you. This is peripheral vision, which we use naturally all the time, but when we aren't totally relaxed we tend to go into foveal vision, where we stare at one thing in detail – rather than peripheral vision where we see everything but in much less detail. In peripheral vision you're aware of everything and everyone in the room even though you're looking at one spot on the back wall

4. Advanced driving instructors apparently encourage people to use peripheral vision because you can take in so much more information, especially tiny movements, in that mode. This means that if your audience members make a tiny movement you'll be able to notice it with your inner mind and then take some appropriate action. Also being in peripheral vision automatically means that because in effect you're "looking " at the whole audience they're more likely to feel included - even if you happen to be facing the other way for a moment while you address a question from the other side of the room for example

5. Become friends with the audience. Now that you've established in your own time how you're standing and the kind of vision you're using, it's time to connect properly with the audience. Bring your eyes down

and begin to make eye contact with individuals, if you need to revert
to focusing on the spot to regain your composure then do so and then
practise bringing your eyes down to meet others

It's well worth practising this with a group of friends before doing it for real. Just
a small warning -when you begin to learn this you may well look a little artificial
and even a little expressionless, but that's OK because you're learning! Keep
going and notice how quiet your mind is when you're in the presenter state. As
you become more comfortable with this technique you can begin to add in more
eye contact and natural welcoming smiles and so on.

The aim is not to have you rooted to the spot and for everyone to become a
robot presenter, but to give you a safety net; a space in your mind, a special
type of vision and way of standing that you can begin every presentation with
and return to whenever necessary in order to maintain or regain control of the
situation. Always give yourself a few seconds to get ready - ensure you're in the
presenter state before you begin your talk; too many people think they have to
start their presentations immediately. Actually a short silence before starting is
a good thing anyway because it draws in the audience's attention to you. This
whole process, once practised, will only take you a few seconds or even less
when you begin to do it without even thinking. Always ask yourself if you're
calm and relaxed before you begin; if not you haven't yet achieved the presenter
state. When you've done it properly, the monkeys will either be silent or very
short-lived as you challenge them and bring them round to your positive new
way of thinking. Now it's time to become more aware of a few other tips and
tricks.

Get your monkeys on your side

"Remember a few of your favourite things"

A great song from *The Sound of Music*! Do you know the one I mean? When the
kids are scared, they're told to remember a few of their favourite things "and
then you won't feel so bad".

Well it's true. Humans are different from other animals because we have the
ability to think about what we're thinking about! We can control our thoughts
because they're ours to control now that the monkey's no longer in charge. If
you find yourself slipping back into old habits, saying or thinking what might go
wrong, then focus on your favourite things instead. Even better, think about how
you'd like the talk to turn out - perhaps people saying "well done!" Or simply the
sound of the audience clapping or perhaps just the feeling of returning to

your seat knowing you did your best. Whatever they are for you – think of your favourite things!

Start to notice how you talk to yourself as you think about public speaking. Ask, "Are the monkeys helping me?". If you want to see great results, then give yourself the best chance! Find positive things for your newly tamed monkeys to say; things that you believe. Even if you aren't quite ready for them to say, *"You're a great presenter"*, then how about, *"You're becoming even better at presenting than you already were".*

Practise these positive phrases in your head and notice how different they make you feel inside.

"Monkey Tail"

Personally I enjoy speaking in front of others - yet all too often I get reminders that I'm not confident all of the time! When I was starting out and a new member of Toastmasters International (a fortnightly group to practise your public speaking skills) they picked me at random to do a two-minute talk on a surprise subject - right there and then!

I could almost see my confidence start to slip from between my fingers! In situations we aren't used to, most of us feel nervous, or not as confident as we'd like. Be OK with that. Despite the feelings inside, I won the Best Speaker trophy and others told me how confident and relaxed I looked. I've learnt how to speak well, even if I'm not feeling confident, so you can too.

Goodbye monkeys; hello monkeys

As you learn to tame the @(O_O)@ and get them on your side you'll start to present and speak more. As you get more experienced you may find that some more monkeys crop up. But you'll notice they're unlikely to be Red ones because you've caught them early enough. Also there'll probably be fewer because you've already cleared a lifetime's pile-up of monkeys.

Also any new @(O_O)@ won't be so intimidating because you know they're trying to help and that you've tamed them in the past so you can do it again. You know you just need to go through the process and get them on your side. Some people, as they get more and more experienced at the process, begin to tame monkeys really quickly and often all at once, but even if we need to do it one at a time - everyone gets much quicker at it.

> ### *"Farewell! God knows when we shall meet again."*
>
> ~William Shakespeare

I still get @(O_O)@, when I do something new or different but once I realize it's a monkey, I tame it within seconds. As you learn the techniques in this programme it may take you a little while to do your first ones but as you stick with it you'll notice you get quicker and quicker.

"Nervous" should be banned from dictionary

If ever there was a case for a re-branding exercise, as we call it in marketing, then this is it! The feeling we have in our tummies before we go on to stage or anywhere to perform shouldn't be called "nerves"; that seems to have negative connotations. It seems less supportive of the overall task we're trying to achieve. That feeling could be seen for what it is - the hormones pumping through our bodies. The hormones are a good thing; they can be used to help us to perform better. I'd like to suggest instead of the "N" word we decide from now on to tell ourselves that we can feel the hormones getting us pumped up and ready for our performance (Perhaps don't say this out loud through for fear of arrest!)

"Monkey Tail"

I discovered a new monkey a little while ago. I went to deliver a bespoke business presentation and my very good friend Rach was in the audience. For a moment a monkey sprung into my mind: "What if she doesn't think it's any good!" Don't worry! I spotted it was a Red monkey and got rid of it really quickly but it's interesting to know they can pop up in new situations – sometimes in the most unexpected places.

Chapter 7 -
Preparation, structure & practice

Now we've taken a look at helpful mindsets, let's cover some tips and techniques for structuring your content and preparing and practicing for your presentation or talk. Let's face it – most people have never learnt to do any of these things, so having a technique that you know works for each step will be more than helpful! There are many ways in which you can approach these things and I want to share some of the best and simplest ways I've come across so far.

First let's look at the preparation side of the presentation – an aspect that's often totally missed by some! Preparation *is* important and, no matter how time-pressured you are, a little preparation goes a long way. In here you'll find some helpful tips on how to prepare thoroughly and also how to create a structure for your talk even if it is at the last-minute!

Consider your audience

One of the first things I ask my mentoring clients before they tell me all about their presentation is "Who's in the audience?" or "Who's your ideal audience?". So many times I see people just open up their laptops and start to write a presentation before they've considered the audience or the structure they need to follow. Many new clients I work with have forgotten that the audience is a key ingredient – they used to be so worried about what their monkeys would say that they forgot to think about what the audience wants and needs.

If it were all about you, then you might as well stay at home talking to the mirror. The reason we get out there and talk to an audience is because we want

---

"Monkey Tail"

I was asked once to teach presentation skills to a group of doctors and I realised pretty quickly as I went about preparing the training that while I have a lot of experience in the world of business, I hadn't had much experience of working with doctors - other than on the receiving end! As I prepared the content for the training, I imagined being in their world and considered what their challenges might be. Next, I went looking in my network for a few doctors so I could gather their opinions. They gave me additional insight into the challenges and on the unique angle from which doctors might be coming. Not only did their input help me to understand my audience better, it also gave me the confidence to know that I had a mini-insight into their world. As expected, while the situations are very different for doctors, the monkeys they had were very much the same as yours and mine used to be!

to have a positive impact on them. If you look at the big picture, it's pretty simple. Understand what the audience wants and give it to them. If you can't give it to them, get as close as you can to giving it to them! If you don't know what they want – find out! Put yourself in their shoes. Imagine floating into their heads and being them and then ask yourself, "What's important? What do I want to know from this speaker?". Additionally you could speak to a few people representative of the audience in advance to get a feel for the audience or speak to the organisers. They will know. Take every effort to get to know your audience. Preparing properly is the key to success.

Set goals for your talk

All talks, however short, are worthy of some goal-setting - otherwise you might get blown off track and forget what your objective is. Use the goal-setting tips in Chapter 9 coming up to help you. You may choose to allocate the time you spend on your goal-setting according to the importance of the talk - but even if it's just a quick talk, just take a few minutes to write down your goal.

How to prepare

If you're asked to give a presentation, do you haul out the laptop, open up PowerPoint and then stare blankly at the screen. Ring any bells?

Always prepare an outline before going anywhere near that software - or better still don't use it at all – see the next section on PowerPoint!

There are many preparation techniques, and what works for me is mind-mapping. Especially if I'm ever stuck for a place to start. Sometimes I find a topic or project can be so overwhelming that I find just putting everything down on paper in no specific order on a visual mind map is a great place to begin. You can use good old fashioned paper and coloured pens or mind-mapping software – whatever helps you to move forward. The key thoughts and ideas form the start of each branch and then related ideas or concepts attach to relevant branches and so on. The shape, colours and pictures all help your brain to work in an effective manner. There is plenty of advice on mind mapping found on the web and I highly recommend you discover more.

As the project or talk starts to take form I might do a second mind map to put the content into the 4MAT® structure which is covered below.

You can then refine the mind map and use it as a memory aid too.

Here's a mind map I created for a 20-minute stand-up comedy sketch:

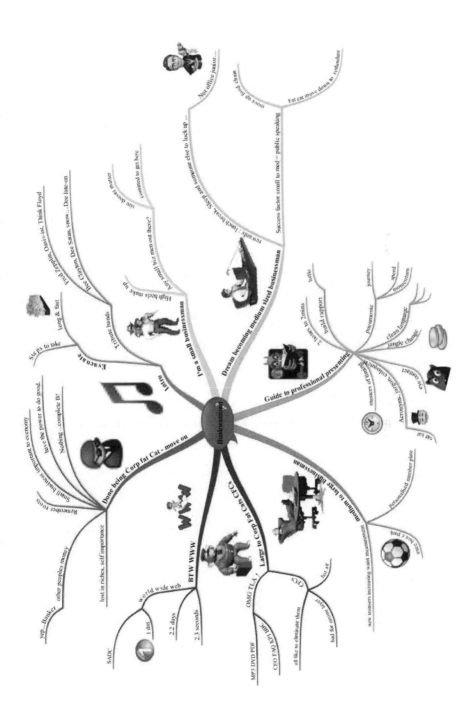

A simple structure for any presentation

The structure of the presentation or talk is really important. The fact that you have all the right "bits" doesn't mean you have a compelling presentation! If you don't present them in the appropriate order, your talk can be at best confusing and at worst rejected or ignored. By presenting information in an easy-to-understand structure you'll see much more success. Not only will you be sharing the information in an easily digestible manner - you'll also be able to see if there are any missing pieces of information from the jigsaw puzzle. I'll share with you a 4-step structure for any piece of communication, so although you'll be using it for presenting here, you can use it in the future for any kind of communication – websites, leaflets, emails, letters etc.

Since being introduced to 4MAT® by Bernice McCarthy (world renowned educational theorist) at The Performance Partnership's "Train the Trainers" course, I've always used it as an excellent structure for most of my communications. I encourage my delegates to do so too because of its amazing simplicity and flexibility (like anything - only once you've learnt it!).

Using this structure, people with all sorts of different styles will get what they need from your talk. You may naturally find some bits less easy than others, so it might not be your preferred style. All the more reason to practise it then, because your audience will likely contain people who suit every kind of style!

This structure is great for last minute preparation too. I went as a guest to a business event once where the speaker still hadn't turned up five minutes before the talk was due to begin because of the snowy conditions. I grabbed the opportunity to speak in his place and used this structure to scribble out my plans on the back of an old receipt I had in my purse. I prepared my "off the cuff" 20-minute presentation within just a few minutes.

There are 4 and a bit steps to the 4MAT® system.

The little introduction

Firstly you need to set the scene with a short and snappy introduction. Of course we want to hear who you are and what you're speaking about but *please*, we don't need to know where you went to university or what you had for breakfast! Just a short introduction will suffice – a few minutes perhaps. The aim of this introduction is twofold:

To build rapport with the audience and make them feel welcome

Little Introduction	
WHAT IF I want to use it for...?	**WHY** do I want to know this?
HOW is this relevant right now?	**WHAT** do I need to know?

To ensure the audience knows the context of the talk or presentation as they may not have read any pre-material or their minds might be elsewhere. This is just a brief introduction to ensure all of the audience is on the same page

Fatal mistake number one: most presentations start off with a 10-minute section on the speaker personally or their company and why they're so amazing. Boring! Personally, I come from the "I'll think you're amazing when you tell me something I'm interested in!" school of thought!

1) Why do I need to listen?

This section answers the question WHY. It gives at least three answers to the audience's question, "Why would I want to listen to this talk?" The audience then knows why they want to engage fully and listen to your talk (Hint: if you can't think of any, change the talk!).

It's your role to give the audience reasons to listen and clearly demonstrate what they'll gain by listening. If the audience have been told to come to the talk it's even more important to cover this bit well. They may have been "encouraged" to turn up, but no one but you can encourage them to listen and be persuaded.

Including both work and personal reasons is sometimes even better. For example I might say that "this presentation will help you to get your nerves and fears under control and, for those of you with children, nieces and nephews, once you've learnt to tame your monkeys you'll be passing on that empowering message to the younger generation too". Hopefully this will mean that even if they aren't motivated enough to do it for themselves they might well want to do it for the sake of their children or others.

Some people are very good at understanding and empathizing with what others want, and some people find it less easy. If you find it less easy then use these questions to help you get a general picture of who the audience are and why they might want to listen to you.

Imagine you're an audience member; really put yourself in their shoes – to do this you'll need to know who you're presenting to. Imagine yourself as an audience member and consider:

- Current knowledge and position along the "journey" e.g. Is this the first time I've heard this idea?

- What external factors might impact on the audience that the speaker will need to empathise with e.g. journey stress, time zones, personal challenges, financial results etc.

- What do I want from this talk? How will it add value to my life? Here are some of the more common motivations people use in this section to help you to get in touch with your three audience motivators

- Save time
- Save money
- Build your confidence
- Save effort and hassle – make life easier
- Keep you informed and up to date
- Give you new information to share with your clients/customers

2) *What do I need to know?*

This is the audience's next question. The answer often forms the main element of the content, covering the facts and information. It's the answer to the audience's question, "What's this all about and what information do I need to know?" This is where all the information goes, the data, facts and perhaps a little of the history etc. I won't spend long on this section – even though this may well be the main part of your presentation, this is easily understood by many because most presentations only consist of the "What" element. They only tell people what they need to know (not why they need to know it or how to use it). You'll need to consider what the audience already knows and the range of knowledge or experience in the room. Consider how you'll pitch information that's new to some people and well known by others.

It's a little harder for me to comment on content unless we're working together personally, but you need to know that you're truly the expert in this area. If you're starting out then you're still more of expert in a specific area than others so just make sure you find your area (e.g. a fresh eyes perspective on the agrochemical industry!). Keep your expert status in mind as you decide what to include in your talk.

3) *How does it work or how can I use this information now?*

This section covers the answer to, "How will the audience use this information - either immediately or in their day-to-day life?" This is all about usability and relevance; it's about demonstrating the talk's relevance to the audience in the here and now.

Here are a few examples of how the audience can see how it works or use this information in a practical way:

- Demonstrate the product or the results (before and after)

- Do an exercise or role play that enables the audience to experience the key points

- Give the audience guidance or appropriately positioned "instructions" on how to use this thing, for example:

  - Use it...in weekly reports

  - Apply these learnings...next time you sign in

  - Pass on information...to the customer

  - Do it differently....use a new process

If you really want to encourage action, you could take the first step with them. This reduces the fear factor and gets them on their way through an exercise, practice, case study or group task.

4) *What if I want to use it for this or that?*

This section is all about answering the audience's need for future relevance. The previous "How" section was about more immediate short-term use, whereas this tends to address the longer term or bigger picture. This is where the questions fit in because this is often an open section where the audience might ask, "What if I do X - will it still work?". Ideally, if you've followed this structure well, you'll have answered the other three types of questions, so you should be left with mostly "What if?" questions at the end of a talk. You can't possibly allow for the wide range of those "What if?" questions, but there are always some more obvious ones you should prepare for.

To summarise in this section, I often finish with a short answer to the audience's question, "What are the future benefits of doing what you're saying?"

- Q&A – (the audience's way to apply the information in their world)

- Wrap up with negative consequences if they don't do what you suggest

- Followed by positive results when they do follow what you suggest

By addressing each of these sections in that order in all your communications, you'll satisfy everyone's preferred style. You'll always have a structure you can follow to put together a talk or presentation – even if you only have a few minutes, you can scribble this structure out on the back of a receipt!

Ideally, create a new mind map following the 4MAT®. Even if the *what* and the *how* take up most of the mind map, remember the *why* and *what if* sections are still important.

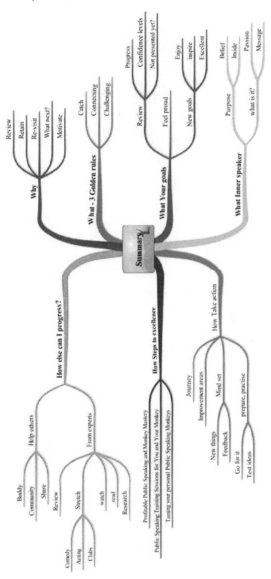

For information on taking this structure from the notes stage into practice see the next chapter.

Bringing your talk to life

Now you have something interesting to say, you want to consider how you're going to communicate it in an interesting way. Here are some ideas I use and I'm sure you can add to the list:

Theme – Any talk can benefit from a theme, especially traditionally dull topics! You know the ones I mean, right? Thread your theme throughout your presentation and then at the end you can decide on the title for your talk. Make sure the theme *adds* to the talk rather than detracts, though!

Emotions – The use of emotion draws the audience into your talk. Remember to keep it positive - it's rare that a very negative story is appropriate. If you're talking about a challenge you overcame, or perhaps promoting charity work, go gently on the negatives – you probably don't want the audience to leave in tears!

Memory aids – If you have points you want the audience to remember, consider developing mnemonics for the key learning points. Mnemonics are often verbal, such as a very short poem or a special word used to help a person remember something. Don't worry, this needn't take up all your preparation time – there are plenty of free tools to help you. Just Google "mnemonics generator" or "anagram generator" and let the web do the work for you.

Visual impact – many people absorb information more easily by seeing it rather than just hearing it so it's important to help your audience to picture things – either by providing a strong visual yourself or by helping to paint a picture in their heads by describing the idea very powerfully.

If you can afford it, getting a cartoon or illustration drawn in my opinion is unbeatable. Cartoons are especially good if the concept is not totally easy to "get" and needs to be communicated quickly. In addition to the monkey cartoons I had drawn, I also commissioned a series of three cartoons (www.landers.co.uk) to illustrate the process of miscommunication and successful communication using NLP techniques.

Within this first cartoon there are many elements of NLP I could teach, for example broken rapport through "mismatching" or different body language, (arms, body stance, and facial expressions!). Clearly the message being sent is not the same as the one being received etc.

Now in this second cartoon as the body language starts to look similar to the other person's, (arms, body stance, and facial expressions) the message being sent is easier for the other person to understand.

The final cartoon demonstrates that only once any communication is understood, can it be passed on within your network, through word of mouth with customers etc.

Humorous stories – Personal stories can be safer than jokes. Because they actually happened to you, you'll remember them and they'll help the audience to get to know you a little better - as long as the story's relevant to your speech and presents you in the right light!

Props – Use a relevant prop that will raise people's curiosity. At the very least, please, if you're selling a product, *bring it with you*. Bring a photo of it, a part of it or at least the results people get from using it.

Quotes – when used wisely quotes can really underline your key points and add another perspective. They're also good for people to remember and take away.

Topical references are strong because they link in to other things the audience has heard elsewhere - but, again, ensure they're relevant. If a huge topical event is particularly relevant to the audience, your failure to mention it might almost break rapport. For example, if the audience has just hit the annual targets and you're a guest speaker you really could benefit from mentioning that as long as you've run it past the client and organisers first.

Many people say that a **strong opening** is important and I think that's true – but consider what a strong opening is. It doesn't have to involve you running out on stage to the *Rocky* theme tune. A well-placed smile and a succinct observation or question can be equally strong openings.

Sweets – Often a winner (unless of course it's a slimming club or dentists' conference). I sometimes bring Jelly Babies and talk about people turning to jelly in front of an audience. Or I have bowls of sweetie bananas and talk about not feeding the monkeys. Make sure they aren't too crunchy and are relevant! (Oh, by the way please don't tell my dad about this - he used to be a dentist!).

Include questions

Do you know how powerful questions in a presentation actually are? Are you already aware of how questions can help? If not, would you like me to tell you? Well, did you know they encourage the audience to become more engaged because questions make you go inside and think? Perhaps you yourself sometimes repeat the question in your head? And then feel you need to answer it? Don't you?

When preparing your talk, you could use questions at the very beginning in order to discover the audience's problems or pain points, couldn't you? Do you think that questions that help you identify how they feel about your topic might be helpful - before you go wading in? For example *"Just so I can get an idea of where we are; who thinks this could work well... (await response) and who still has some outstanding questions... (await response)?"*

Do you have any questions so far?

Some people ask me, *"Dee how can you make sure the audience will raise their hands and join in rather than just leave you with an awkward silence?"* Perhaps you could benefit from the following:

1. For the first few questions, ask ones they're likely to agree with and say "yes" to

2. Clearly and obviously raise your right hand as you ask, "Yes?" (This indicates you want them to do the same). If you aren't totally confident with this movement the audience will notice and won't commit to it fully

3. Wait for a response. With a British audience you may need to cajole a bit here but it's worth it because from then on in they'll interact with

you. Be honest or make light of the situation if it helps to get them to answer you. E.g. I might say, "I really want this to be an interactive seminar and the only way I know how to do that is to measure the response I get from you – so when I get a nod and a hands up I know you agree (I nod and put up a hand); if I get a blank face I know I need to explain something a little more clearly or a head shake may suggest you don't agree. Is it OK for you to give me that feedback?" (Nodding at the audience!)

4. When some of the audience start to raise their hands and engage, nod at them to encourage this. If not everyone has agreed, offer them an opposite or different choice and put up your left hand

5. For example, I often say, *"Do you feel nervous when you're speaking in public?".*Then I put my right hand up and say, *"Yes?"* in a questioning tone and nod at them until they follow. I might then say, *"Or do you feel pretty confident when speaking?"* and raise my left hand

6. Once you have shown the audience what to do once they'll know what to do from then on in.

There are some other techniques too, though they're even more advanced, so I won't go into that now or we'll never finish! Do you think now that it will be really powerful to combine your message with great questioning ability? Does that make sense?

Addressing the audience

When you address the audience remember it's full of individuals - not a rabble. Each audience member's an individual so it's much more powerful if you adjust your speech accordingly. Because we see a group of people when we look into the audience, there's a temptation to speak to them as a group. It's not wrong, but if you're up for an advanced challenge, there's an even better way. Speak to them as individuals. That's how they're processing your talk inside their heads.

Read both of these paragraphs quickly and see which one's speaking to **you** more effectively.

A) *"You know how important it is to improve your public speaking, don't you? Good. It's important to build your confidence, so you can experience more success and continue to improve as a speaker. Now you know that, are you interested in taking your skills to the next level? Do you want to become even better?"*

B) *"Who here knows how important it is to improve their public speaking? Good. It's important for everyone to build confidence and then you can all experience more success and continue to improve as public speakers. So who here is interested in taking their skills to the next level to be even better?"*

Which did you feel spoke to you more directly? I hope you're thinking A. So, when you're planning your talk, learn to appreciate the power of one.

Keep it simple & focused

You know your product or service inside out...every feature, every benefit, every section and every scenario. However, if you're trying to convey too much in your talk you'll be caught waffling or going off topic. Your audience will very quickly become uninterested and wish they were somewhere else!

Unless you're talking to a room of experts, don't use trade-specific language or "shop" talk. If you have to, then give definitions for your terms. Remember the point is NOT to show off how much you know (unless that really is the goal you set yourself!). Get your point across in a well-structured and simple manner and your audience will leave knowing you're a master of your subject.

Like you, I've sat in on too many presentations that were factually correct yet didn't answer the original brief...so please **stick to the point!** The key here is to keep in mind the brief or the reasons why you're presenting in the first place. Of course you won't have that issue because you'll have ensured that the brief was well understood before you actually planned the talk and the structure follows the 4MAT® system!

In any presentation, it's good practice to repeat the key messages at least three times and often more. Think of how often a song needs to repeat the chorus in order for us to remember the words. Think of the key messages as the presentation's chorus, often being revisited throughout the talk

---

> **... it's good practice to repeat the key messages at least three times**

Speaking at other people's events

I strongly recommend that you seek opportunities to speak at other people's events if they're relevant. But when you do, watch out - always check with the person asking you to speak what they need and want covered. Of course, what they *think* they want and what they actually need are not always the same thing! Make sure in your preparation that you sense-check what's being asked for - you don't want to be stuck giving an untargeted presentation. I have on several occasions worked with organisers to amend the angle of the talk - and sometimes to change the brief altogether. Remember, you want the whole event to be successful - so do anything you can to help it be a success and then you'll be invited back next year.

Now that we've taken a look at some helpful ways to prepare and structure the presentation, the next steps are to practise the presentation.

Practice

After good preparation, practice is key – even if you don't have ages to do it. I'll show you a short cut - how to get as much done as possible in a short timeframe. Practice is not only about delivering the presentation, but also about knowing the environment you'll be speaking in and remembering to have all your props and tools ready. There are some things you might never have thought of, so use my online checklist at **www.deeclayton.com,** which will be continually updated with new ideas as you submit them. Search on the website for "Presenter's Checklist".

Once you know what's in your presentation "Practise, Practise, Practise" your presentation with a friend, colleague or buddy to help you become more comfortable. Check and ask for constructive feedback in the feedback sandwich - then use the information to improve your presentation. There's no point in practising a poor presentation - that won't help!

Some of the content might change - as you practise it you'll see ways to improve. That's OK - treat it as an organic process that improves over time.

Practising and notes

Some people read from their notes, with their head down, rushing to get through as quickly as possible. If you do need to read from your notes (and I don't recommend it), then look up at your audience frequently. That makes it more varied - and at least you'll know they're still awake!

If you need notes, here's a technique that works well, so you don't just wind up reading from them:

1. If yours is the kind of talk that needs scripting and writing out in full then do so. Otherwise go straight from the 4MAT®mind map suggested earlier into step 2 below.

2. On index cards, write your key points down. Use at least one index card per part of the 4MAT® e.g. one index card on "Why" maybe four on "What" three on "How" and one on "What if" You could even colour code the cards to match the 4MAT®structure

3. Write no more than three points on each card and no more than two words per point

4. Accompany each key point with a visual that reminds you of that point

5. Number each card in case they're dropped so you'll quickly be able to re-order

6. Practise using your cards and time yourself until you are confident

7. Practise without your cards – referring to them only when needed

8. On the day, only take your index cards with you – leave the script at home

9. Trust you know your speech - with a little help from the cards to keep you on track

This works every time people use it. The only challenge sometimes is helping people to adhere to the rules of three points per card and two words per point. When they don't, I rip up the index card and ask them to re-write it. There's a reason why I'm so strict! People who follow the rules end up with clear thinking and an easy-to-follow set of cards. People who try to get away with writing their script out again but on index cards often end up with a muddled mind and a muddled speech. Then, if they need to refer to their notes, they've no chance of finding where they were because they're so busy and unclear! Keep notes clean, simple and brief – you only need a few key words and phrases to help you stay on track. After all, you know your subject inside out!

Then leave the cards to one side while you're speaking - near a glass of water perhaps - and only refer to them when you need them. If you need to be able to see what you've written quickly and easily, just head over to the glass of water and review your notes briefly while rehydrating!

The visual is not everyone's favourite bit - some people start telling me about their drawing monkeys (Well you can guess how to get rid of those can't you?). Anyway, you don't need to be able to draw – just to scribble down a clear visual of something that reminds you of the key word or phrase you need to remember. Don't make it complicated – keep it simple and literal.

Example of a good index card

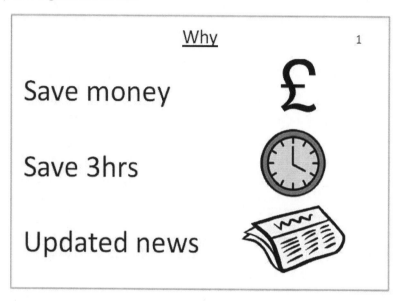

Trust the process

The best way to approach a talk or presentation is by taking full responsibility for everything and doing as much as possible to ensure it goes well. Then be OK with it not going perfectly! You've done everything you can; you've covered your bases, but something still might happen that's totally out of your control, in which case it's your responsibility to be in the best frame of mind with the @(O_O)@ on your side. That way there'll be plenty of extra room for you to come up with lots of possible solutions or talk yourself through some options.

Let me use an example:

If a piece of equipment failed perhaps in the past it could have sent you over the edge and made you panic - but now you've sorted out the monkeys there's a new calmness inside and you'll be able to think on your feet about a solution. You could ask someone to help you mend the equipment while you carry on talking. You could use hard copy hand-outs instead of relying on the projector. There are always many ways of overcoming mistakes, errors or incidents. The problems only occur when the speaker's not in the right frame of mind to address those challenges. Now you'll be able to call upon the help of your newly tamed @(O_O)@ to help you stay in a resourceful frame of mind and have access to everything you need to continue with the presentation effectively.

How to remember your words

I'm often asked, "How should I remember my words?" and mostly my answer is "Don't!". I much prefer teaching people to use the index card method. When you know your big picture 4MAT®structure and the key points you need to communicate within that, you can naturally complete the rest. As long as you keep to time and it's a topic you know, after some practise you can trust your inner mind to fill in the spoken word competently. After all, you do that every day. I assume you don't normally write out your daily conversations word for word before having them, do you?

The benefit of this approach is that it allows your natural personality to come into play; lets the talk be conversational and friendly in style yet structured and professional too.

However on certain occasions and for certain types of speaking you might need to learn things word for word. The first time I came across this was when I needed to learn my 20-minute comedy set. Because of the work I do on preferred communication styles I'm well aware of my preferred communication style for learning. There's much more to learn about this interesting area, but for now consider whether you learn better by:

- visualizing things – seeing pictures or words in your head.
- hearing things – talking out loud or to yourself, or listening to others
- feeling and doing things – being practical and hands on, good at learning physical things

Ideally, a combination of all these things will be a great way to learn.

Primarily I prefer to learn by talking through things and hearing things. What I did was:

1. Record my set word for word onto my voice recorder, using the tonality, pauses and speed that I thought was most appropriate.

2. I then listened to it several times in the car or whilst walking, even as I was going to sleep.

3. Once I felt I knew it fairly well, I'd talk through it at the same time as the voice recorder and pause it when I felt the answer wasn't immediately coming to mind. Either I then remembered the answer or I needed to play the answer to discover what it was.

4. After a few times you'll begin to notice that there are a few areas that you don't remember as easily as the rest. And this is the magic time saving advice...

5. Practise only the bits you need to! Identify the parts that aren't going as smoothly as the rest and ONLY practise those. This might mean that instead of taking 20 minutes to practise the talk once through, I can now spend a few minutes practising a few bits ten or even twenty times.

6. Where appropriate, only practise the connector words. What I MEAN by that is that it probably isn't even the whole paragraph or joke that isn't working; it might just be the start or the end line or often the transition between one thing and another. (See Monkey Tail below for an example of this)

7. Draw up your final index cards with key words and matching visuals, using those as you practise your final run-through of the whole talk and notice how well it all comes together.

"Monkey Tail"

I still remember the line and the lead-in that I specifically needed to focus on learning for a new comedy sketch over a year ago. My joke was about TLAs (Three Letter Abbreviations) and the set up was about how you should avoid using them where possible.

The lead-in that I needed to remember was connecting the previous end line of the last joke to the first line in this joke, which looked like this: "...all like to eliminate them. I did a report once..."

First I focused on just making the two jokes link together. I used a visual in my head (a picture of someone being shot and then having to write a report on it) plus a hand movement (making a gun of my fingers and then turning that into holding a pen and writing) along with repeating the line out loud.

Next, I worked on remembering the following line, which I didn't find easy: "I did a report once for the CEO of the BBC answering FAQs about KPIs. It's available to read if you want on MP3, DVD or PDF." I found focusing on learning those two things was very quick once I knew specifically which small bits to focus on. On the night, I delivered really quickly as intended, word for word, and received a round of applause along with the all-important laughter.

Hand-outs

By giving them hand-outs, you ensure the audience can look at a specific visual for longer or make notes in the presentation at a relevant place. I'm in favour of a brief visual given to the audience before the talk. Yes they might read it while you're speaking. Good! Isn't that the point; that you want them to take in the information? It's not our place to say the audience must be looking in your eyes to be listening to your message; they might find it easier to take in when they look at visuals in their hand or write notes. Of course, it isn't always possible or practical, but hand-outs do cater better to some people's learning styles and pace. Always keep them to as few pages as possible in order to communicate your message. While it isn't very environmentally friendly, I haven't yet found a suitable substitute.

Stay on time

ALWAYS practise and time your talk by speaking out loud or delivering it to a buddy or friend. Ask them if the speed was OK. Giving your talk to a live audience is the best way to know how long it will take; you need to allow time for nods, thinking, responses and perhaps even laughs (in the right place!). A mirror just isn't the same!

I often use a free standing digital timer – the same one I use in the live presentation – that way I become practised with the workings of the timing device too.

These days with the technology of voice recorders, either hand held or on your PC, it's easy to record yourself. As you listen back to your talk, re-write anything that's not easy to say. See where you need to add more emotion or additional interest points.

Stories add to any talk

As you run through your presentation, start to see where you can maximise the use of stories or mini-stories. Your whole presentation will be one whole narrative, moving from the beginning to the middle to the end, perhaps with a mix of emotions as you move through the presentation. Be aware of which emotions might be present in the audience and when. Think about whether you want those emotions or if you want to influence them to feel something else instead. For example, a presentation on change management might leave many people nervous or fearful. You may want to demonstrate empathy with those emotions and also ask the audience to point out any positives such as seeking out new opportunities.

Why are stories so powerful?

- ✓ People love stories – we're used to hearing them all the time. News stories, bedtime stories, people's stories

- ✓ They're the preferred communication of the unconscious mind

- ✓ We talk in stories every day: "Well you'll never guess what happened but..."

- ✓ Stories allow the listener to interpret the message, so the writer or speaker can guide the audience to a conclusion, allowing the audience to complete their own details

- ✓ Stories are more memorable than plain facts and data

- ✓ Good stories are emotional - often an emotional roller coaster. Think of your favourite movie, book or piece of music. Isn't it your favourite because of the way it makes you feel? Does it have that feeling all the way through? Or does it fall and rise and perhaps finish with a dramatic ending?

- ✓ As a speaker, when you begin to tell stories the audience often listen transfixed as they start to go into a difference space where they're relaxed and calm

- ✓ As a business speaker, you'll want to make sure you tell relevant stories that flow easily and have a point. For example, customer testimonials are stories

- ✓ Use a selection of descriptive words, describing what the scene looks like, what sounds there are or what people sound like and what feelings are present - or use the words to help stimulate the desired feelings in the audience

- ✓ Change your voice to match the story, making its volume appropriate and using your voice to be expressive

- ✓ Remember, a good story, like a good presentation, has a clear beginning middle and end, and has characters or people we can relate to

✓ A good story also has curiosity and suspense. The WHY section fulfils this purpose quite well. It gives a teaser to the audience as to why they should listen and then throughout the presentation slowly reveals the story or facts

✓ Finally, keep it simple - never overload the audience, keep it to the key points and then re-iterate those so they remember. This way the message really sticks

> ## Stories are more memorable...

So we've spoken about your mindset and body language and preparing for your talk – the things that can happen prior to the event. We've practised it and we know what we want to say. Now let's take a look at actually doing it and, of course, gaining valuable feedback after the event.

Chapter 8 –
Delivering the talk and feedback

This chapter gives some pointers on delivering the talk on the day and how to approach it, including my views on PowerPoint®. We also talk about the value of now being able to hear feedback in a balanced and helpful manner instead of having it tainted (often in a more negative light) by those pesky monkeys.

PowerPoint®

Don't be like everyone else. Don't assume that everyone else is doing it right because often when it comes to PowerPoint® they aren't. Do use PowerPoint® only to <u>add</u> to what you want to say.. Here are some tips to doing it well:

1. Consider whether you need to use it at all – if you need to illustrate something often flip charts can be much more spontaneous and interactive

2. Ensure that each slide has a purpose. A great book to help you get the slides looking good, among other helpful tips, is *Presentation Zen: Simple Ideas on Presentation Design and Delivery* [Garr Reynolds]

3. Use a consistent look throughout the presentation whilst avoiding a company template that takes up half the screen with your logo before you've even started

4. Ensure the text colours are easy for the audience to read, especially when they're projected onto a screen - I tend to stick mostly to black on white

5. Vary the visual ways in which you communicate your message as mentioned earlier e.g. use cartoons, bullet points, quotes, photographs, statistics, graphs etc.

6. Face the audience, not the screen. This often happens when presenters use the presentation as their *aide memoire*. PowerPoint® is not the same as notes (see earlier point on notes). If you aren't yet ready to throw your notes away completely, use index cards or anything else except PowerPoint® – it is not a prompt

7. Did you know that on a PC when you're running a slide show you can enter the "Number" of a slide then "Enter" – to jump to that slide?

8. When presenting, stand out of the way of the projection onto the screen. As nice as your silhouette is, it can get a bit tedious across 20

slides! Hint: if the light from the projector is shining in your eyes you're in the way of the screen!

9. In between slides - or when not in immediate use - avoid projecting a company logo on your chest by pressing the "B" key (when in slide show). On a PC this will make the screen go Black. Press any key to return to the show

10. I've been told these work on a Mac too and if you need further help you can press the HELP key during a slide show to see a list of keyboard shortcuts. (The HELP key is not available on all laptop keyboards.)

11. Ensure you're plugged in – it's not great when even your computer falls asleep!

12. If you can, use a remote control clicker to make slide changing look seamless. If you don't like them, stick to page down until you get more confident. BUT don't get stuck standing by the computer. Walk around the stage and return when you need to click

13. Always have hard copy hand-outs you can give to the audience if the projector has a hissy fit

14. Take a copy of your presentation on a USB stick in case you need to use a different computer. I often save it as a PDF so that I know formatting issues won't occur between computers

15. Remember, the start of the presentation is when you create your first impression. If you can get the equipment @(O_O)@ quietened down by being prepared, you'll be able to concentrate on giving a great presentation!

16. Never rely solely on the projector - see it as a bonus if it all works OK!

While we're on the topic, I highly recommend this hilarious sketch on YouTube by Don McMillan: **Life after Death by PowerPoint®**. You really must watch it – it will make you laugh and also reiterate in your mind why it's good to follow best practice!

Room layout

It's your talk and you're in charge of making sure the audience gets the best result.

Make sure the room is how *you* want it so that you can best deliver that result.

Here are a few pointers that will help:

- Always ask about room layout before you arrive

- Illustrate how you want the room laid out and send it over to the venue or organiser

- Visit the venue prior to the talk. Get a picture in your head of the room and decide whether PowerPoint® is needed

- If you haven't booked the venue yourself, you might need to speak nicely to the right people at the venue to make a few changes. Be patient and persistent

- If there's a lectern there, ignore it or better still get it removed! Let us see you!

- If you expect 30 people, set out 25 chairs and have spare seats around the room (Better to give the impression of a popular talk than leave empty seats)

- Always arrive early. Often the room won't be laid out as your diagram showed! It also gives you an opportunity to test the equipment

- When you think you have it right, sit at the front and then the back of the audience and get a feel for what it's like looking towards the stage

- If it doesn't feel right, change it

- If you're using technology this is all part of your surroundings, so make sure you know where everything will be...your screen, your keyboard, your pointer or mouse

- Where's the microphone? Will it be hand-held or attached to your lapel?

- Preload your presentation on the computer and projector you'll be using and look through every page to spot formatting errors

There's so much more I want to share with you, such as how to make your talks

> ## If it doesn't feel right, change it

even more memorable by using key words, key phrases and the rule of three. Or how to make your talk titles engaging so your seminar's fully booked, or how to use your hands to paint a picture for your audience and how to use the stage to communicate time-frames or how to use powerful and positive words. All this and more is covered in Step 2 - Public Speaking Training Sessions for You and

Your Monkey, which I referred to at the beginning of the book. But I'm already running out of pages and we've yet to actually stand and deliver!

Confidence time travel

Are you any good at time travel? Sometimes we need to fool our minds into believing something ahead of time so that we actually start to believe it in the here and now. For example, a good approach is to believe in yourself and then act confidently ahead of time (do a bit of time travel) so that your body gives off the body language of confidence and then the real feeling of confidence follows. As the real feeling of confidence follows – you start to believe you are more confident!

It works because your body and your mind work together. So if you convince your mind to think your body's confident, then the feeling of confidence will soon come. Try it now. Stand up tall, shoulders back, head straight and legs hip-width apart. Keep your back straight and notice you find it harder to lack confidence in that position.

It's perfectly normal if you feel slightly apprehensive before a presentation but it won't help if you tell the audience that. You'll just be feeding the monkeys more bananas and it might make the audience nervous for you! Some people feel this is a bit like a safety blanket: *"Oh well, I told you I was nervous!"* Don't do it! Don't give yourself an excuse not to perform to your best ability. Pretend you're confident ahead of time, stand as if you're confident, feel your feet firmly grounded with the floor and the confidence will follow.

 I also believe you can be *over*-confident in your abilities: being so sure that all will go well that you don't prepare or even think about your presentation or audience in advance can cause problems. Almost all the best speakers, comedians and TV presenters do prepare their materials; they at least have a structure and goal, even if they then act as if they're delivering them "off the cuff". What I'm assuming is that anyone working on this programme first wants to lose their nerves and fear and then to move on to be a good and strong communicator and speaker. In my experience, it's best to have matched your confidence with your skills.

Voice

Women tend to have naturally quieter voices then men, so make sure the volume's loud enough. Older audiences also might not have the hearing they used to, so be sensitive to the audience's needs.

When I work with clients who are *really* quiet, I sit at the back of the room and ask them to keep speaking louder and louder until I say stop. That's when I know it's the right volume for the audience. By that point they can't believe that's appropriate. They think they're almost shouting. Ask your presentation buddy to do a volume check with you! Remember your idea of the volume is irrelevant – what matters is whether the audience can hear you.

Vary your voice: it's never good to sound dull, disengaged or tired. Bring in a bit of energy because if you don't have the passion and enthusiasm for your topic you can't expect your audience to. As you become more confident and bring in emotions and stories into your presentations you'll find your voice naturally becomes more varied. Again, ask a presentation buddy to help give you feedback or record your voice and listen back to it – ask yourself if there are areas that need improvement.

Vary your speed

You can speak quickly to get across information, but slow down if you look like you're losing your audience. It's not a race to say as many words per minute as possible. Use pauses, and remember to breathe. Taking control of your breathing will make a huge difference. If you start to speed up, take a deep breath, then a normal breath, and then continue. If you're wearing a microphone - make sure you do your breathing quietly!

Using voice speed is a great way to bring variety into talks, whoever your audience. You can slow down for the dramatic bits or speed up when you're conveying excitement or passion. Watch out, though. You don't want to speak too quickly all the time. You'll need to slow down if you look like you're losing your audience - sometimes it's better to say less but be very clear on the key points.

"Monkey Tail"

I've trained in Brussels many times with an audience of international trainers. I learnt that I needed to slow my usual pace right down. The participants were covering totally new material, they needed to translate it into their own language, get over any personal challenges they had with the subject comprehension and then consider how they would train it onto their delegates when they rolled it out in their countries. I needed to give them plenty of time to do all those things so I slowed down, added plenty of pauses and continued to watch the group to see when they finished writing. Then I continued to the next topic.

The power of pauses

Any type of silence might seem to last a lifetime to you when you're speaking, but actually pauses only **add** to the audience's experience. Don't rush through your talk. Pauses will:

- Give the audience time to **absorb** the information

- **Emphasise** the key points in the minds of your audience

- Make you look **confident**

- Give you time to **plan** what you're saying next

If you need gather your thoughts then do so. It's better to take the time out to get back on track than to waffle on hoping you'll find your place again!

Some "umms" and "errs" are natural and that's OK

Some people say you need to get rid of all filler words - and if you want to be a great speaker that will be another thing to aim for. If you're happy being a good speaker then the filler words, when not over-used, make you come across naturally to the audience. If you're prone to using specific words way too much (including "so", "OK", "basically" and the like) you'll want to focus on improving this area because it can be very distracting for the audience. Leave a silence instead or slow down to gain the valuable thinking time you need to formulate the next line!

The thing is, most people who have this problem have absolutely no idea they're doing it because they're so used to it - and more importantly because they've never asked for honest feedback. Another good reason you'll want to ask your buddy or a friend for constructive feedback on a presentation! Alternatively, the video never lies!

Body language bloomers

Common body language "Off Putters" are swaying, pacing, hand flapping, pen fiddling, leg crossing, (yes, while standing up!) and –possibly the worst for women to watch – pocket change rattling. Avoid temptation - men take your change out of pockets and find another place for it, after all how much money do you need to give a talk? Ladies (and some men) – consider your jewellery. Jingly bracelets, long earrings or dangly medallions can be very off-putting for the audience in more ways than one! Wear simple studs and well-fitted jewellery items.

Remove any jewellery you find tempting to play with - such as watches or bracelets - before you stand up to speak. If pen lids are your thing, leave them on the table when you get up to talk.

"If it doesn't add - it distracts"

So my comedy tutor Logan Murray used to say

When you practise, ask a friend to point out where you could be even better (notice the language again). Ask them to word it exactly like the example below and you'll find it easier to make the improvements:

"What I would like to see is your feet remaining still" or "What would be even better next time is if you were to keep your arms relaxed by your side".

Ask your buddy to say what they DO want to see more of – it works better that way.

Movement

It's often more engaging to watch a presenter who moves their body in line with the story being told. The problem comes when it's distracting. Add energy and spark, but don't fidget or pace across the stage. Learn how to move well and with volition.

It's OK to make mistakes

I always talk about the belief that there is **no failure; only feedback.** You may have heard other people say this too. What is a mistake, anyway? It's just something we didn't plan, didn't prepare and perhaps would prefer not to happen.

If you say something you wish you hadn't you'll know for next time that you'll do it better. If things don't go to plan, you'll know that you'll be able to deal with it in a humorous manner another time.

The audience truly is very forgiving. They won't mind if you do make a "mistake". BUT if they feel that you're uncomfortable with what's happening, if you get in a flap about it, it might rub off on them too.

When I've seen speakers make fluff ups, it can make me feel more connected with them anyway. *Phew – they're just like me!*

"Do not fear mistakes. There are none."

~Miles Davis

A secret trick if you really, really have messed up, is this...

- Step away from the point where you made the mess up

- Point to that place and say, "I can't believe I said that!"

- Return to your spot and continue as if nothing had happened

- Never refer to it again

It will either be totally forgotten or not remembered it was you who said it. Only use this once and reserve it for really BIG mess ups!

Q&A and discussion sessions

As you heard when we covered the 4MAT®system one of the styles is to learn through asking questions. Did you know that?

Prior to knowing and realising this, I used to think the "Questions" section was just a formality. Now I realise it's an essential part of the training or talk. It's good to encourage and welcome questions and well-managed discussions. Here are a few ideas so your session goes smoothly:

- **Tell the audience** up front when you want to take questions

- Take questions at the **end of each significant section**. If someone doesn't understand something now, it might frustrate them to wait until the end to ask

- **Ask for comments and thoughts,** not just questions. That way it becomes more interactive as the audience shares what they've learnt

- In your preparation, **consider some of the obvious questions** that might come up and have an answer prepared

- Always ask *"Does that answer it?"* or similar after you've answered, of the person who asked the question. Especially if it's a bit **complicated**

- Allow sufficient time for questions. Have someone primed in the audience to get the questions flowing if you need to. There's no need to ask artificial questions, just ask them to have their own question ready, should you need it

- Manage the time for questions and discussions so you don't cut someone short. e.g. "And I have time for just two more questions, so in the last minute let's just quickly hear from Joe!"

- If you have a **microphone**, repeat the question before you start to answer it

  - ✓ It ensures you've understood the question correctly

  - ✓ It allows the back of the room to hear the question asked

  - ✓ This gives you time to gather your reply

Does that help you to improve your Q & A sessions?

Take charge

In any group situation, someone will always take the lead. For your sake - make sure it's you. Own the stage. Tell the audience what you want to happen and when.

If you want to get the room to pay attention at the start, stand upright and still, looking at the audience and smile. The room will gradually start to hush. You must mean it and stick it out. It may take a few minutes the first time you do it, but it's worth it. The next time that audience sees you do that very thing, they know what you want to happen.

Listen to other speakers

If you're part of an event with other speakers it's best to listen to the others before you go on. This has multiple benefits:

- You can adapt your talk to fit in with what the audience may have already heard

- You can hang on the coat tails of success – if someone earlier mentioned a popular topic you can carry that theme on into your talk and build on it

- There's always more to learn from other speakers

- If you really don't have time, ask someone to give you a brief summary of what other speakers' key points will be

- If you refer to something someone else said but you didn't hear it yourself always turn it into a question, just to be safe. E.g. "I think Susan talked about Management Development, didn't she?"

Managing mini monkeys

If you do hear some mini monkeys when you're just about to present, that's OK; use all the tools you've learnt to date to challenge them and they'll melt away. If you notice a new one that's not been totally dealt with yet, then either tame it there and then on the spot or, if it feels like a gorilla, promise to address it straight after the presentation or that evening, in return for its leaving you alone for the moment. Beware! You can only use this once – the monkeys must be able to trust you and know you're a person of your word. They've done a deal with you to let you do your talk well today in return for your listening to the monkey soon after. Don't ever try to trick your monkeys - they're wise and they will return next time more powerfully if you don't pay them the attention they want when you promised!

Feedback

With the monkeys on your side, you'll now notice that feedback consists of two key elements:

- How good the other person/people think you are

- How good you believe you are

The ideal is to get those two measures aligned so that you *are* good and you know it. And where you aren't so good you know it too and do something about it if you choose to.

Always use the feedback sandwich discussed in Chapter 3 immediately after any practice session or real talk (You might need to re-read that little bit now). It's imperative that you continue to get balanced and helpful feedback that says both how well you did and what else you can do to continue along your journey to becoming a great speaker. Remember you can ask other people to give you feedback in the sandwich and also ask your newly tamed monkeys to use this approach too! I use feedback forms on my course and I've designed them around the feedback sandwich so that I can maintain my motivation by hearing about the things they loved and also feel good about any suggestions for improvements. One of the things I like to think my business does really well is respond to feedback and strive constantly to improve. That doesn't mean that you bend with every suggestion someone ever makes, but it does mean you evaluate the feedback without bias and decide what's the best approach for the client or audience.

Already you've done really well because very few people take the time and energy as you have firstly to overcome of their fears and then secondly to learn some excellent techniques and approaches. I've shared techniques that great speakers have been using for decades in the areas of:

A. Your mindset & body language

B. Preparation: structure and content

C. Practice

D. Delivery

E. Feedback

So far you've read all of the tips and techniques - so you're probably more knowledgeable about speaking techniques that work than most of your peers and probably others too because most people just avoid speaking or muddle through doing their best.

Review your progress

Whether you've been reviewing your progress as you've been working through the book, or you've not reviewed yet, now's a good time to take a look to see how far you've travelled and recognise your achievements.

By looking at what you have written down, you'll be able to see how far you've come. That's why it's so important to write things down - otherwise there's a tendency not to remember what you said you'd do! Then, as you progress and achieve things, you forget to recognise all your achievements, which is important. Now, if you aren't someone who likes recognition then that's OK, but if you do like it but aren't sure if it's OK to get it – that might be a monkey, a bit like ones I used to have, saying, "Stop showing off!" or, "You're not all that!". Tame it!

I guess there are two points here:

1) Make sure you notice and recognise all your achievements. Doing this is very motivating to your inner mind. Like small children, if you genuinely praise the monkeys they'll continue to do all the good things you've asked them to and help you achieve even more success.

2) Once you've noticed your achievements, it's much easier to share them with others in a relevant manner. It didn't take me long in business to notice that even if you were a genius, if you didn't tell people how good you, your product or service was or why you were better, you weren't going to succeed. Having recognised your success, you can use that recognition to promote yourself or your department or business in an appropriate and effective manner too.

Well done on achieving some of your aims or some steps towards your goals. There might be some goals you've yet to achieve but they're probably looking much more achievable. For example, if your goal was to "present confidently in front of the team" you may not have actually done that yet – but you have a feeling and a knowing that you'll be confident and far better than you were before and know it's achievable now.

Updating your goals – essential maintenance

This section comes with a health warning – if you don't update your goals you might end up becoming stagnant, with no direction. But when you do update your goals now you'll be able to achieve wonderful new things you'd only dreamed of before. The next chapter takes you through this process. As you go through Chapter 9, consider what you really enjoy doing. What is it you have a gift for? What strengths do you have that you think are "normal" yet which others are amazed by? Who might you want to inspire and what message do you want to share?

Without your monkeys and with some new skills, perhaps you just want to be able to present without fear for the rest of your life. Or could you dare to believe you could become a team leader, a senior manager or CEO of a multinational company? Maybe you'll set yourself a sales target or turn your hobby into a business? Maybe you'll speak on behalf of a charity no one's heard of or rally others to hit a fund-raising goal? Maybe you'll find a hobby you love and stop working so much or join a poetry group and read your poems aloud. Perhaps you want to try your hand at being an after dinner speaker or a stand-up comedian. Maybe you want to sing, dance or join the local amateur dramatics group. Perhaps you want to teach children to be more confident. Whatever your dream, ask yourself, **"What do I want to do with my new-found skills?".**

What do I want to do with my new-found skills?

Chapter 9 –
Why is goal-setting important?

I want to encourage you to do some thinking about what you now want to achieve from your speaking. Instead of just remaining an OK speaker do you want to grow and develop – to help you to achieve greater things? Who knows, you probably don't even know yet as you haven't had a chance to think about it. The next chapter gives you time to think about the future and all these things you've always wanted to do but felt held back in before. The process I take you through is very thorough and detailed for a reason – I know it works! So if you've had ideas of starting a business, teaching your kids how to tame their monkeys, changing career, supporting a charity, starting a club or new hobby, becoming the in-house mentor, becoming an after dinner speaker or speaking up for those that can't be heard or anything at all then spend some time on this chapter.

Everyone says it's good to set goals but most people don't - so why bother? Setting goals - and in particular excellently worded goals - provides you with the motivation to do the job even if the going isn't always easy. Goals also help you to clarify your direction and at least highlight if you aren't totally clear yet on the destination - and finally goals can give you good milestones from which to keep track of your progress. The following section is written with the purpose of speaking in mind but when you apply this to other areas of life too you'll see an amazing difference.

Motive

Motivation does many things; it's like the fuel the engine needs to keep it driving down the motorway in the right direction. Without fuel, after a period of time, you'll slow down and eventually stop before reaching your destination. You need to get in touch with your motivation for speaking so it can keep you going through any more challenging times.

Direction

Goals are also a means of direction. You may have enough motivation and drive and energy to keep you going along the roads and motorways, but if you're heading in the wrong direction you're in trouble. In fact you might not even notice you're lost if you don't keep track of your location! I meet many business people who are racing along at the speed of light, busy, busy, busy, but when you ask them where they're going they can't tell you.

Measuring milestones

Measurement is essential for achieving and celebrating success. It can be all too easy, once you get the tools and techniques to do things, to get so busy that you tend to forget how far you've come in a relatively short period of time. I'd say I'm driven to achieve my longer term goals and if I hadn't written down some in-between goals or milestones then I'd have forgotten how well I'd done or even forgotten to look to see if I was still on track or not.

Remembering how well you do isn't about vanity or showing off to others, it's an essential key to success. It's telling your inner mind or monkeys how well you've done so that it - or they - can repeat that behaviour. Good feedback's very important for repeated success.

Just like children, monkeys like to be told when they've done well - and once told, they'll more likely repeat that success in order to get more praise. We know all this already, don't we? We do it with kids and dogs but we think when we grow up our minds work in a different way. On the contrary, they work in the same way but we just have more knowledge! And that can be a good or not so good thing. We have more knowledge of people and things failing so we might pick up less helpful beliefs... but when you were a kid, didn't you think you could do anything?

Keys to reaching your goals

Goal-setting should really be called *how to reach your goals more often* because we've all set goals before – and it's often reaching them that's the challenge!

Always write your goals down

Just writing your goals down means you're already way ahead of most people! So, if you haven't already, go ahead and write your goals down now! Even if you aren't quite sure this process will help you to tighten up your ideas. You may have heard stories about Harvard University studies where the students who wrote their goals down now earn more than the rest of those in their year put together. Whether that story is fact or fiction, the learning points are still valid. For those that like proof though, in his excellent book *The Psychology of Influence and Persuasion,* Robert B. Cialdini cites no less than 22 scientific experiments demonstrating that where people had committed to something they were more likely to believe it and thus take action. In addition, when these commitments were made publicly, the likelihood increased yet again. So if you want more success, write your goals down, and then tell select people about them.

Think BIG goals

Already you know I love the study of NLP. Fundamentally it's based on a process called "modelling" or copying strategies that have proven successful. When I attended a goal-setting session with David Shephard, a Master Trainer of NLP (with whom I did all my NLP training), it really crystallized the theories from previous learning and experience. It seemed to take goal-setting to an even more advanced level for me.

That coincided with the realisation that when allowed to, growth follows an exponential curve, not a linear one. Planning in a linear manner is not always logical, yet I often see people doing it. This is because of the monkey spirals. As soon as you get on the upward spiral you'll begin to accelerate your success, and as you get more confident and more able to take on feedback you'll continue to improve exponentially. It may take a little time and energy to get the spiral moving in the right direction - but once you're on track it's well worth staying there and enjoying the ride!

Setting advanced SMART goals

SMART

- S   **Specific and Said in the positive**

- M   **Measurable**

- A   **Achievable with Action (by you)**

- R   **Realistic and with Respect**

- T   **Timed and as if it is TRUE**

S   Specific

This is the What and Why. **WHAT** are you going to do, have or achieve and **WHY** do you want to do this?

WHAT are you going to do, have or achieve?

An example WHAT could be, *"I want to speak with confidence at a seminar for experts in the field"*. The next step is to ask yourself, "What actually is confidence?" or "What kind of seminar would that be?". Does that mean you'll have that feeling 100% of the time or just that if you begin to feel less confident you always turn it around to confidence quickly? Will you not use a single note or look at the prompt once or will you just feel like you always know where you are within the presentation structure and always in control of the direction in which you're going? Continue to ask yourself the WHAT question until you're satisfied you've reached a very specific goal.

Think of a goal for your next step on your speaking journey. What would you like to achieve? Then look deeper into the bigger goal behind that. If you want to do more seminars for example, what is it that drives you to want to do them? I believe all of us have at least one important message we want to share, which could be in business or personal life; a fascinating insight or some business learning. When we tap into this, we tend to see more success; we know why we want to put the effort into moving forward and becoming a strong communicator. Spend some time writing down what you want to achieve.

WHY do you want this?

Next ask *"Why"*? This uncovers your motivation. What does *"Speaking at an expert's conference"* enable you to do? For example it might mean you can become more visible and get promoted or sell more. Ask yourself if the thing it enables you to get should be the goal - only you can tell what level of specificity is right for you.

When I've set goals previously it was easy to say, "I want to speak at three events" and pop that down as the goal. Now I realise I need to be clearer on the WHY. *Why* do I want to speak at three events? Maybe if I want to reach 300 more people with my message I don't necessarily need 3 events it might be 1 or 10!

HOW are you going to do this?

Interestingly something I was putting into my goals that doesn't need to happen is the specific HOW are you going to do it. Yes, you need to have a "big picture" HOW e.g. by spending time on practice or by learning advanced techniques, but you don't want to become too specific, otherwise you might be limiting the many different ways in which you can achieve your goals.

For example, I may want to do 10 talks, but if I say, "to groups X Y and Z", by doing that I might not be allowing for anything else to crop up. I've unintentionally told my inner mind that there's only that one route. It might be better to leave it open and start to work on the developing the speech. Then if another route comes along as I progress I'll be ready, able and open to taking it. To make this point I sometimes encourage people to take a look back at the goals they've already achieved and notice how some of them actually came about through something they could never have planned for or couldn't have expected.

S   *Said in the positive*

This is a good rule for life too - say what you *do* want, not what you don't.

Some people are really clear on their goals and others of us need to spend time considering what they are before we really know. I'm still refining many of my goals; I see it as an ongoing process; as I learn more about myself I refine my goals. The most important thing is to have goals, go for them and then review and measure your progress along the way.

> ### *"What you choose to focus your mind on is critical because you will become what you think about most of the time"*
>
> - Noel Peebles

M   *Measurable*

Measurable is exactly what it says on the tin. Sounds simple, right? However, looking back, I found it was only too easy to think my goal was measurable but not really be able to measure it!

A great test is to see how specific your goals are is to answer this question:

"How do you know you've achieved your goal?"

One answer might be: *"I know I've achieved my goal because I can see... hear... and feel..."*

While these are quite "touchy feely" measures, you'll still be able to know whether or not you've achieved them. I'd suggest adding in some more solid measures too - for example: It's December 20th and:

- Audience feedback scores have increased from 60 % "very good" rating to 85% as measured by...

- I've presented to over 100 people in my target audience, which is...

- I've made time to practise my presentation and receive valuable feedback three times before I speak at the conference.

A   *Achievable*

You'll want your goals to stretch you slightly and you need to feel you can achieve them. Being totally confident and monkey-free on your first ever customer presentation regarding a multi-million pound deal, and with very little preparation time *is achievable*. It has been done. Notice that achievable and realistic are not the same thing. You may be thinking that is not *realistic* - and I might well agree - but it *is* achievable.

Remember that when allowed, growth will be exponential so make sure your goals are stretching enough. You might want to break your big objective into smaller chunks and see that it's possible to achieve these smaller chunks over the weeks or periods. Setting **smaller** milestones along the way will help you see more clearly what's achievable and you can measure how well you're doing along the journey too. Just beware not to over-measure - because you need to allow exponentiality a chance to develop. (See TIMED)

> *"Shoot for the moon.*
> *Even if you miss, you'll land among the stars."*
>
> ~ Brian Littrell

Often I find it's at this point where those interesting little negative voices pop up. This is where a new monkey might try to prevent you from moving forward. Although the belief may not ACTUALLY be true, we often FEEL as if it's true. You can probably spot them fairly easily now you've been through this process. Here are some examples of some monkeys when it comes to next step goals: "You can't run a seminar" or "No one will want to listen to you speak."

For years I believed I couldn't draw (A belief possibly brought about by the art teacher at school handing me some tracing paper!). A few years ago I attended a "drawing made easy with NLP" workshop. Within three hours we could all draw well. We had learnt the basics and I drew a pretty good version of my own hand. I am now happy to draw a few diagrams or cartoons in my seminars that make complicated models easier to understand. However, I also realise that to become good would require a significant amount of time, practice and commitment. So now I know I *could* do it, but I *choose* not to do it often!

Even if you've done plenty of self-development and got rid of a bucket load of monkeys through this book, it's likely some more will pop up as you move forward to new challenges and things you've never done before. Take that as a sign you're moving forward. You may want to take note of any new monkeys that pop up during this goal-setting process and work on taming those too using Chapter 5's techniques again.

A   Action

Decide on an action and then carry it out, such as planning and developing a seminar or speech. Then, as you take action, assuming you've left your goals open enough, other opportunities will pop up, such as perhaps an invite to do keynote speeches. So don't get too hung up on taking exactly the right action, just take action in the right direction and then start to learn and adapt.

> *"Iron rusts from disuse;*
> *water loses its purity from stagnation...*
> *even so does inaction sap the vigour of the mind."*
>
> ~ Leonardo da Vinci

Another point to note is that it needs to be your action. You can set goals for other people, but you don't want to come to a dead end if the plan with that person doesn't work. Consider this goal: *"It is Dec 20th and Doris has written a great speech."* To make it work your goals have to be either actioned by you or 100% your responsibility. So if Doris can't do it for whatever reason there needs to be enough flexibility in your goals to ensure you can find another way to get there.

So a better goal may be: *"It's Dec 20th and my award-winning speech has been written."* There are a number of reasons why this goal may be better:

- The WHAT has been written, not the HOW

- The WHAT is clearer - you want it to be award-winning which is more measurable than "great"

- Now Doris, or someone else, could make the goal happen

R   Realistic

This means **"do-able"** for you. If you're stretching yourself enough with your goals then you probably won't know HOW you are going to do it yet, and that's OK. Ask yourself these questions:

1) Do you believe you CAN make this happen?

2) Do you believe you WILL make this happen?

You want the answer to both these questions to be 100% yes.

After all, if you know of people who've done what you want to - then if they have, you can. Can't you? It's just a matter of how determined you are. Remember if you come across any less helpful beliefs or monkey voices preventing you from setting that goal, write down what the monkeys are saying and tame them. You want to be able to answer both questions with a 100% yes, and after more monkey taming that should be possible.

Only you can know if it's realistic for you. Remember it's **your** idea of realistic, not anyone else's! Beware the *"Oh you can't do that, dear!"* syndrome from well-meaning friends and family, which may plant doubt where there was none. You may want to be careful whom you share your goals with.

R   *With Respect*

This is probably what some people might see as ethical. You'll want your goals to be respectful to the world we live in, the community, your family and friends and also yourself. Apart from the morality of this statement, this will ensure that all forces are on your side and will help you to achieve your success in ways you'd never imagined. If you choose to work on goals that aren't either neutral or of benefit to the environment or people around you then you may find people or things get in the way of your progress. To some that might mean not taking all the hours up with preparing for a presentation, but doing enough practice, and then spending some quality time with the family. Of course we all have our own version of what's OK or appropriate. Only you can decide if your decision's OK within what you believe to be important. As a general rule of thumb, if it feels wrong to you, it's probably clashing with your personal values - so take the hint!

T   *Act as if it is TRUE*

> **"Whenever you are asked if you can do a job, tell 'em, 'Certainly I can!' Then get busy and find out how to do it."**
>
> ~Theodore Roosevelt

Another advanced goal-setting technique is to think about your goal and then state your goal with total certainty that it's going to happen.

Perhaps think about it as if you just need to put the steps in place to catch up with it over time. So when you're phrasing your goals you may want to write them like this: "It's June 30th and I'm a confident and successful expert speaker who...".This may seem a bit odd at first, but test it out and see how well it works. You don't need to tell others you're doing it this way if you don't want to! You can act as if you need to catch up with that achievement in time.

Initially when I came across this concept it seemed a little odd. Now, the more I embrace it the more success I experience. Your inner mind prefers it like this because it likes things in the present – it's not so good at thinking about the future or past, so phrase your goal in the present tense and act as if it's already happened.

Now just to be clear, this doesn't mean borrow the money that you plan to make in the future! No! But know a wise investment when you see it, especially if it involves learning. The quicker you learn what you need to know to move up to the next step, the more success you'll see. In my first years of setting up the business I was very serious about learning more and investing in myself. I spent over 350 working day equivalents attending trainings, working with experts and learning new skills. Let alone the books I've read or the many great things I learn from my clients! So you may want to set out clearly in your goals what kind of a person you need to become in order to achieve those goals.

"Learning is not compulsory... neither is survival."

~ William Edwards Deming

T   Timed

Without a time limit, there's no urgency for your inner mind to start taking action now. The time element needs to be measurable, attainable and realistic.

Once you get into the goals you may need to move a few of the timings but at least you'll be doing it for a reason. You'll want to set the goal and then remain flexible enough to move it if needed. Don't move it as an excuse to do nothing, but do allow for unexpected opportunities and new directions.

One final point is to work on finding the right balance between measurement and timing. Remember, growth is exponential, but only when allowed to be. If you plant a bulb in the ground, you trust that in the spring, given the right conditions, the first shoot will show through and turn into a beautiful flower. You don't go digging up the bulb every week to see how it's getting on. Do you? So yes, measure, but also balance that with faith. Continue to act as if you'll achieve your goals even if the shoots haven't yet started to show through.

There is a caution though; I must say this isn't necessarily the easiest or fastest way to write goals. I found it has taken me some time to get used to this new approach to goal-setting. To be honest, there have been quite a few re-writes to get my goals "correct" according to my new learnings. However, comparing the initial time taken up front to phrase the goals correctly and clearly versus the rest of the year spent trying to reach the goals, I realised it was worth the investment and I hope you do too!

I'm sure there's still more to learn about goal-setting and I just wanted to consolidate my learnings in once place to help you to set some really solid speaking goals, both as part of the journey you'll go through while reading this book and of your continued growth as a speaker. Well done on spending some time considering your future, for making your goals Specific and Said in the positive, Measurable, Achievable and accompanied by Action; for checking they're Realistic and created with Respect, stated as if they were True and set against a Timeframe.

I'd love to hear about what you have planned for yourself and your community now your monkeys are under control and confidence growing. If you want to share your goals and story to help inspire others please search www.DeeClayton.com for "Goal Setting Stories" and add your "comment".

> ### ... versus the rest of the year spent trying to reach the goals, I realised it was worth the investment...

In the final chapter we pull together the thoughts and learnings from the previous chapters and I share my thoughts around "finding your inner speaker". We also take a look at your next steps, because speaking well is often seen as a journey, not a destination. So if you want to keep moving forward and achieve your goals I'll share a few tips on where to go next and what additional programmes I can offer you.

Chapter 10 –
And finally...

You've now successfully learnt how to tame your monkeys – ten out of ten, congratulations! After reading the Tips and Tricks section even the few remaining Green monkeys that just needed a little advice and guidance are a lot happier. You don't need to remember all of the Tips and Tricks section - it's always there to refer back to when you need it.
I hope in the Goals section you really set yourself some motivating next steps to keep you moving forwards - so now would be a great time to re-grade yourself on the confidence scale between 1 to 10 where 1 =no confidence at all and 10 is very confident, relaxed and looking forward to the next presentation.

Your score may vary depending on whether you've actually been presenting as you've progressed through this book or whether you've been reading it first and are now planning to go and present.

If you've been presenting as you've been reading the book you'll have experienced the improvement in practice or "real life". You'll have noticed the feeling of things becoming easier and easier. You might have experienced a monkey-free presentation or only a few mini monkeys popping up occasionally but with almost no impact on you because you now have the confidence to manage the little fellas. Any mini monkeys are nowhere near the size you felt they were at the beginning when you were reading Chapter 1. Yay! You've been Dee-monkeyfied!

If you've been postponing, avoiding or waiting until you finished the book to present then now's the time. You've learnt the techniques and processes and you feel inside that your monkeys have diminished or disappeared – that's great. Or you may be the kind of person who needs to really see it in action in the "real world" to prove that this works. That's OK too and the very reason why you <u>must get up to speak as soon as possible </u>(more on that later).

Tell 'em what you're gonna tell 'em, tell 'em, then tell 'em what you've told 'em.

You'll have heard before that in presentations it's a good thing to tell 'em what you're gonna tell 'em, tell 'em and then tell 'em what you've told 'em. Well this is me telling you what I've told you! Firstly, well done on getting this far. Now all we need to do is pull together all the strands so you can review everything you've learnt already in your own mind, improve your long term retention of what you now know and allow your mind to consolidate its learnings. You'll want to revisit any relevant areas, such as your goals for example. Once we've briefly done that together, the rest of this chapter will look at the next steps into the "real world" and what the future might look like as you progress on your speaking journey.

The journey began with you deciding to take action to overcome once and for all the fear that was holding you back. You learnt that "nerves" or the feeling of hormones rushing around your body when you were in **a new situation** was natural. But because of the negative monkey voices in your head, you used to get your wires crossed and a little confused. You were introduced to the **Taming the Monkeys** process, which has helped you to untangle those old connections and put more helpful ones in place.

We learnt about the importance of having big picture motivations that you're passionate about to help you overcome any bumps through the process. If, for example, you weren't feeling motivated to do enough prep for your next speech, or you weren't finding it easy to find the time to practise, then you know the first thing to do is review or revisit your answers to the motivation questions. When you continue to set clear and well-worded goals, you'll notice that they **motivate you** more than enough to move you into action. When you have powerful goals they make it all worthwhile, bumps and all! Review and refresh your goals often.

We covered the Golden Rules:

- ✓ Catch them
- ✓ Connect with them
- ✓ Challenge them

We took a look at Georgie's monkeys and how together we tamed them, before you went ahead and tamed yours. When you **caught** your monkeys, you acknowledged their presence and identified each monkey -giving each one the long-awaited attention it desired. You no longer ignored them and just hoped that they swing off of their own accord.

As you separated them into individual @(O_O)@, you started to realise that you could communicate with them. No longer were they a huge faceless gaggle, but individual monkeys wanting to communicate with you, each with their own thing to tell you.

As you began to **connect** with them using Golden Rule #2, you realised they were there for a reason: trying to protect you - but from something old and out of date that happened all those years ago.

We looked at the **monkey traffic lights,** splitting out the Red monkeys  (total ridiculous fibbers) from the Amber @(O_O)@ (who had a negatively exaggerated view with some small truths). We then discovered that the Green @(O_O)@ were good and actually really helpful - rather than be concerned by them, you now know that you just listen to them and either decide that their comments aren't important or take action to learn how to address their concerns.

The last step was **challenging the @(O_O)@** and by the time you got to this Golden Rule#3, you might already have noticed that some of the smaller @(O_O)@ had been befriended or disappeared completely. It was time to challenge the Red and Amber monkeys because they were totally fibbing or out of date. These monkeys were harping on about an event – perhaps only a tiny event in your life, which nowadays you'd hardly even notice (or might approach very differently).

The problem came about because monkeys have long memories and sometimes group unrelated things together. Your monkey was still trying to protect you or avoid something that happened ages ago I expect. It's OK to know that the way you felt was totally normal but that the monkeys just needed a helping hand to "grow up". The main outcome of that process was realising you needed to address the problem by understanding how you held the old problem in your head. Then you questioned the monkeys' version of the "truth" using the "Challenge the Monkey" questions. These helped you to rewire your monkeys and overcome any battle in your head.

The questions were specifically scripted so that whether you realised it consciously or not, they took you to the heart of the monkey. Reading through a couple of the examples before you did it yourself probably helped because it often seems easier to see other people's challenges before your own. Those questions will always be there for you to refer to in the future should any mini monkeys pop up. I still use those questions to this day to eliminate any mischievous mini monkeys, but since I'm experienced at monkey management it takes only a few seconds.

There was a warning about monkey trickery, how sometimes they can be so cunning they try to convince you to avoid or swerve the questions. That's when you might have found it helpful (and, more fun) to call a buddy in to help; someone who held you accountable to answering those questions, even if you'd not been working with one before.

In Chapter 6 we looked at mindsets and one of the most common ones I see is the worry about making a mistake. I just want to remind you of the process

I support: Firstly take full responsibility for everything in your talk, and do as much as possible to make it go perfectly. Check out the room ahead of time; get to know the audience, look at the speakers' checklist online. Write your speech, practise and get feedback - do everything you can to make your presentation go perfectly within the time frame or priority focuses you have.

The next element is to be OK with it not going perfectly. Despite perhaps wanting to, you can't control everything. You've done everything you can; you've covered your bases but now the best thing to do in order to increase your chances of success, is to make sure you're in the best frame of mind. If something doesn't go quite to plan, you need those @(O_O)@ on your side, with extra space in your head to come up with possible solutions or think through your options. Then, most importantly, commit 100% to the best course of action and look for audience feedback to see if that solution's working. If not, try anything else until you get the result that you want, all the time maintaining your calm and confident manner.

We looked at a potential equipment failure as an example and how it's pretty much guaranteed that you'll get a better result when you're in the right frame of mind to continue the presentation effectively.

Finally, in the last chapters we covered helpful hints, tips and techniques to kick start your new successful speaking journey. If you want to know my top three favourites, which I've seen can transform any presenter after their monkeys have been tamed, they are:

1) Your approach to feedback. As long as you have the most helpful approach to feedback you can always learn and continually improve by spending practice time on only the RIGHT stuff for you to be practising.

2) Presenter state so your mind and body are in the right place – literally

3) The 4MAT® structure for presentations so the content's right for the audience and also clear in your mind so you present confidently

Don't stop me now...

Your journey isn't finished yet; in fact for some it's just beginning. For those who decide to go further and take the next step, now there's no fear to hold you back. Will there be an element of fear at the next level of your journey? Maybe - but even if there is, you have the skills and techniques to overcome that fear. Don't let the "change isn't easy" monkey prevent you from moving forward to learn new things. Now you have the confidence to know that you've overcome your fears in one area, of course you can do it in more! Yes, you may need some help and support - and the secret is knowing where you want to get to, and why. The how you get there will then take care of itself - you'll find the help you need once you're focused on what it is you want.

Remember, I'm not saying you won't ever get monkeys again - I'm saying you have all the tools you need to tame any new ones that pop up as you push yourself to achieve more.

"Monkey Tail"

A little while back, having never been really nervous about presenting, I decided I needed to know what it was like for my many clients who felt extreme anxiety when they stood up to speak. While the tools and techniques always worked, despite my not having been in the situation, I felt I could be even better at empathising if I knew more about what my clients were going through.

So, like any sane human being, I signed myself up for a comedy course! As I went to the first of several sessions I was pretty nervous. Even when we had to introduce ourselves, which I've done a million times before, I felt a huge pressure to be funny. My "You're not funny" monkey was paying me a visit. I kept thinking I must say something humorous about my name like, "Yes I'm the youngest of 4 children - the first born was called 'A'...."

Unfortunately even that gag was borrowed from a funny guy who compered for us on a tour of Australia when I worked for a major wine company. He was a brilliant host and I remember wishing I could be more like him and just come up with funny and clever things off the cuff. Well of course now I know that he had loads of practice. He wasn't just born that way; he was passionate about it so went on a journey to make himself good at it; so good that people were happy to pay him for his skills.

I used this very technique to tame the monkeys and just got up and did the best I could. A significant part of being a stand up is being OK with just giving it a go. Some will hit and some will miss, but that's the only way to learn.

The Speaker Within

Once they've tamed their monkeys and reviewed their goals, clients often begin to get in touch with the speaker inside themselves. This is the part of you that has something important to share with the world, but which perhaps has been buried until now. Some people are crystal clear on what it is after the goal-setting section and others haven't fully discovered it yet, but just know there might be something more. Having seen many people go through the process of discovering their inner speaker, the first thing I want to share is that it's a hugely rewarding process. When you find it, some people have described it as a huge physical connection between you and your message, combined with that emotion of finding a long lost friend. It's possibly harder to describe what your inner speaker is, other than that for many of us it's a journey rather than a destination.

It all sounds a little hippie-ish but as you begin to get on the right path you might feel an inner sense of knowing that this is the right thing. When you talk about it you might find you become passionate and light up; you can start to see it all fall into place, and the path just seems to unravel in front of your eyes. You won't feel as if you're pushing water uphill but that the right opportunities come your way and as long as you're clear on your goals and open minded enough to take unexpected opportunities. You might even find it an easier path than you'd ever imagined.

"Monkey Tail"

When I was an employee in big corporate organisations with household name brands (and as a marketer) I was more than happy to tell the sales team, the customer and the world how good the brand I represented was. When I then discovered all these fabulous communication tools that relatively few people had heard of, I decided to start my own company sharing my new-found knowledge with business people, to help them achieve more success and follow their goals. Initially it wasn't easy. What I hadn't accounted for was how much of my personality or identity I had attached to those brands or the job roles I used to hold. When I left, I remember for a while really questioning who I was and what I was about. I used to be Marketing Manager of Jacob's Creek wine, which is something most people can understand, and now I was just Dee Clayton. Who's she? I used all the tools of the trade I'd learnt to help me discover what was important to me and therefore what that stood for as a business and brand. Although they're constantly developing, I'm now crystal clear on my message and purpose.

I tell you this because I see this pattern in some of my clients, for example mums who've stopped their careers and whose children are now flying the nest: they don't know who they are anymore or what their purpose is. The same goes for people who've retired early. It sounds fantastic but without a clear purpose it can be a little daunting. People who've been made redundant may feel the same – all sorts of people, in fact. If you aren't sure who you might be underneath, perhaps it's time to tune into your inner speaker!

My "inner speaker" is all about transforming myself and helping others to be the person they're destined to be (I warned you it was hippie-ish didn't I!). The more I follow this path, the more successful and fulfilled I become. I was just about to say that I didn't always know my path, but that's not true. When I look back I can probably see the clues leading me to this road, but I let other things get in the way: the fear and concerns, the doubts and limiting beliefs in my own capabilities. Yet I also know that everything I've done in the past has led me here and will continue to take me on my journey, which I thoroughly enjoy. Now

I help others to overcome their fears so they can uncover their path and add value to the world.

There are so many elements to discovering your inner speaker but here's one quick exercise I love to get you started. I'll tell you why it's so special after you've done it.

Exercise – inner speaker

Answer off the top of your head and write down your answers to the following questions; it's important that you do this quickly - both questions must be answered well within five minutes, so start the clock!

Q: IF YOU WERE GIVEN THREE MINUTES TO ADDRESS THE NATION AND SAY ANYTHING YOU WANTED TO, WHAT WOULD YOU SAY? WHAT MESSAGE WOULD YOU WANT TO SHARE?

Q: WHAT'S IMPORTANT TO YOU ABOUT THAT MESSAGE?

This is only one of many tools to help you find your inner speaker so, depending on what you came up with, you may well have surprised yourself. I hope you have!

Stand on your feet and speak from your heart

"Monkey Tail"

I completed this exercise over five years ago and only recently did I appreciate its power.

My answer all that time ago when I was really at the early days of realising I wanted to step up and do something more was:

"I would tell people that they're often so much better than they think they are; that they should believe in themselves so they can achieve more and make their world a better place."

Now I'm not saying that was the most articulate answer I could have given but my point still holds true.

Shortly before finishing this book an odd thing happened, which sprung from left field. I actually was offered the opportunity to "address the nation" – well sort of! I was invited to be interviewed on ITV News at 10, a nationwide news channel that has an audience of around 3.5 million people, which is about 10% of the UK's adult population - now to a "Brit" that's what I call an audience and my biggest one to date!

Technically speaking, the interview wasn't in my niche area – it wasn't about presentation skills. Being inquisitive, I spoke to the interviewer to discover more about the topic. The piece was about inequality of pay between men and women and, as an entrepreneur who used to be in the corporate world, they wanted my view. I briefly ran my view by her, which I knew was controversial but also something I believe in - so the worst that could happen is she'd say no. But equally if she liked it, it would secure the interview – always good to have an opinion in the world of PR!

I know inequality happens but if women just accept it they will feel powerless to do anything about it. My point was that women can also help themselves more by:

- Knowing their value and the worth they bring to the organisation

- Becoming more confident and comfortable SPEAKING ABOUT their successes

- Asking for what they want - such as promotions and pay rises

In other words getting rid of their monkeys that hold them back!

The special correspondent loved my angle and confirmed that I should come to the studios to be interviewed immediately. Of course I had some monkeys, which you can read about on my blog, (search for "TV Interview") but I tamed them quickly on the train, and when interviewed for 10 minutes with the camera staring at me the answers flowed easily. Of course I was edited and it became my "15 seconds of fame" but I was very pleased that my core message remained intact. Even more interesting was that the special correspondent, who must interview hundreds of people a week, emailed me to say she thought my interview was inspiring. High praise indeed! The more connected I become with my inner speaker the more "opportunities" seem to come my way.

Here are my key learnings from that tale, which I wanted to share with you

- Trust that opportunities will arise – remain open

- Stay focused – encourage your inner speaker and message to evolve

- Once you know it, make your message easy to understand

- Stand on your feet and speak from your heart

Wherever you want to go next with your speaking, it might be easier than you think

I'd like to share a secret - It's relatively easy to be a good speaker because few people decide to overcome the fear and nerves in order to improve. So before you go judging yourself too harshly just know that there are many people with the same old fears and nerves you had, but they haven't tamed theirs. They may have a certain image to uphold or they're embarrassed or they feel it might affect their careers or business if they ask for help. Since you're one of the relatively few who are determined enough to complete this process, I have no doubt that with a little practice you'll become a good and maybe great speaker.

How good or great you become really depends on the underlying skills you have. Some people are naturally great communicators or have learnt to communicate clearly to the best of their ability in all sorts of situations. If the @(O_O)@ were preventing you from accessing these skills then yes, there's every likelihood that now you have tamed them you'll be able to access those skills and use them to the full.

If your goal is to be a great presenter and this is important to you but you don't have these skills - you'll almost certainly need to learn them. After all, if you've been totally avoiding speaking for a long time you won't have had as much experience as others. But that's OK because with your @(O_O)@ tamed you're in a better position than most to learn new techniques and approaches easily and effortlessly.

Step 2, which I mentioned earlier - "Public speaking training for you and your monkey" - would be a great next step, as would other opportunities to improve your skills and get balanced and supportive feedback on your presentations. So, if I may, I want to share a little detail on the next two steps to speaking excellence you can take with me - then I'll give you some other ideas and you can choose which are best for you.

Public Speaking Training Sessions for You and Your Monkey (Step 2)

I say these sessions are Step 2 because you've already completed Step 1: "Taming your Monkeys". These sessions take your skills to the next level now you've got rid of your fears, and they're designed to guide you through the next stage of the game - getting on your feet. After all, if you've been avoiding speaking for a long time you may have a bit of catching up to do! Of course, you can learn through practice, reading and more study, but these sessions enable you to turbo charge that process. Firstly I share with you how to uncover your personal learning style so that everything you learn comes to you more easily. Then I take you through the basic and then advanced steps to becoming a confident, strong presenter.

The sessions involve learning effective speaking tips to ensure you deliver your communications with confidence and passion. We focus on the practical changes in the way you approach presenting. We apply and practice the tricks of the trade with proven techniques, including a more in-depth application of those techniques shared in Chapters 6, 7 and 8 including examples of using the 4MAT® structure in presentations, how to optimize your body language and get rid of any distracting habits. We also go deeper into audience interaction techniques while remaining calm and confident and keeping those @(O_O)@ at bay. We even start to look at how to get those newly tamed monkeys helping you!

The programme helps you to learn new techniques and then gather feedback from your own "real life" presentations wherever practical or at "home practice" sessions in front of friends or a video.

The sessions are most often conducted through teleseminars, on line tutorials, videos and regular webinars . There are various programmes available so there'll be one to suit your needs and your budget, each with associated differing levels of personal one to one feedback.

To get your free personal development report, which uncovers what you personally need to focus on in order to take your skills to the next level, email dee@deeclayton.com with "free personal development report" in the subject line and simple instructions will sent to you.

Profitable Public Speaking and Monkey Mastery Mentoring (Step 3)

Mastery enables you to get to the top of your game. It's not for everyone and only some people are committed and focused enough to take this step. I've designed it for business leaders and those in highly visible situations, or people who want to free their inner speaker. Individual mentoring and coaching is available.

During the intensive one to one personal sessions and throughout the programme you'll receive the keys you need to achieve your goals, which will include everything we cover on the Public Speaking Training sessions (Step 2) plus:

- ✓ Maximising your personal learning style

- ✓ Mentoring programmes uniquely tailored to your needs so you only focus on the problems and challenges you are grappling with

- ✓ Light-hearted sessions with constructive feedback helps you implement and embed learnings quickly and is proven to "stick" better!

- ✓ Accelerated learning with no time wasting covering only relevant topics. We'll use techniques that work in the real world to develop repeatable approaches that once learnt, will remain long into the future.

- ✓ Flexible and discrete timings to fit your schedule

- ✓ As a marketing & communications expert with experience across sponsorship, PR and TV advertising, I will enable you to package your messages effectively and memorably.

The topics will depend on your needs but other mentoring clients had covered areas, such as:

- ✓ Motivating and inspiring teams

- ✓ Establishing yourself as an expert

- ✓ Learning how to stand out in the crowd

- ✓ Learning how to find your personal or company gap in the market

- ✓ Expressing your unique selling or buying points

- ✓ Learning how to promote your seminars, talks or presentations internally and externally.

What we cover will depend on what you need, so if you're interested please contact me personally by email: Dee@DeeClayton.com referencing "Mastery" or call me on the numbers shown on the www.deeclayton.com website.

In addition to these sessions I also offer:

- ➢ In-house training tailored to company objectives, including project presentations and customer pitches

- ➢ Limited availability open courses for individuals who want to expand their speaking skills "toolkit" and practise in real life.

- ➢ Free hints and tips on my blog at www.deeclayton.com/blog

- ➢ Free updates, latest thoughts and exclusive offers when you sign up to my newsletter "Monkee Mail"

To support you in making the right decision, (subject to fair T&Cs) all one to one programmes come with a No-Quibble Money Back Value Guarantee

Continue learning the topic of speaking

When we talk about continuing to learn, some of my clients tell me early on they haven't studied a new topic for a long time (some feel they haven't learnt since school). They need a bit of guidance about how to learn. By learning to learn you'll not only improve your speaking abilities but also pick up all sorts of new tools to improve your skill sets. You'll have your own favourite style and techniques as well as those I share with you in the next steps, but here's one of my techniques:

- Decide on the one topic that you want to focus on for a period of time. Pick one that's relevant to you and your goals; something you're motivated to learn about. Suppose you have a long presentation to remember and you want to improve your memory techniques - you might search on the web for "public speaking memory techniques" or just "memory techniques" and apply those learnings to the field of presenting

- Look at the experts on the web or elsewhere and differentiate the real experts from those who just say they are! I like to find people who give interesting angles and new thinking rather than just repeat old information that may not even be factually true. For example whether you like Derren Brown or not you have to admire his amazing memory ability

- Look for books or articles you want to read, audio you want to listen to and videos on Youtube. The problem is not really how to get the information because there's so much available; it's about sorting out which experts you want to learn from

- Allocate a time frame to decide on which sources you're going to use e.g. two hours' research to look through reviews and recommendations or skim-read parts. Within that time, I tend to have narrowed it down to maybe several videos and articles and five books on a topic

- Allocate time in your diary to spend on learning – it might be 30 minutes at lunchtime every day, an audio while you drive to work or something you read at bedtime. Just pop in regular time and you'll get through it easily. Remember, not all books need to be read cover to cover - you can skim read or photo read books or just read the chapters that interest you, knowing the other chapters are there if you want them!

- Mind-map your learnings from all the sources as you go along and decide whether you know enough to reach your goals or see if there are any gaps that need filling. What will probably happen is that during the course of your learning you'll have found a new area you want to learn more about so you'll want to repeat the process. Soon enough, you'll find yourself an expert among your peers on those topics you have studied.

If you don't know a good place to start on the topic of general public speaking, I recommend a website called "Six Minutes" (http://sixminutes.dlugan.com), which seems well-archived and packed full of interesting information from a range of sources. Once you've done this, please feel free to share your learnings with me and our online community - tell us about experts you've found to be great and their areas of specific expertise so we can all learn together. Search www.DeeClayton.com for "Other Public Speaking Experts" and add your learnings in the "comments" section.

Continue learning the art of speaking

As I mentioned earlier, being a speaker is a continual journey - I strongly recommend that you continue to learn the art of speaking so your communications keep improving. Now you've tamed your monkeys it's likely you'll be at least an "average" speaker, if not a good one, so you could scrape by with a good presentation. But if you don't strive to improve you might get stuck, which isn't recommended because in a competitive world it's to your benefit to overtake your colleagues. A few months down the line, when you continue to develop, they'll be looking and listening to your presentation saying, "What the heck happened? When did he/she get to be so good at presenting?".

Now I know it's not politically correct to talk about competition because we're told the competition is only with ourselves - and to some extent I do believe that. I mean, you want to be a better public speaker because it will expand your skills and grow your confidence. However, the real world of business is competitive too. When you present your services, your products, your ideas and yourself better than the competition you're more likely to see more success.

When I work with the charity sector I often hear, "Well we're different - we aren't competitive", but unfortunately the real truth is that most charities are in competition. If you give 5% of your salary to one charity, that chunk of money has gone, so surely you're less able and likely to give another 5% to a different charity.

Other people tell me they "aren't in sales" or that they "don't want to sell". But I've got news for you: we're all "in sales". Even if it's selling an idea or vision, you're competing for airtime. With so many messages and millions of emails and tweets etc. literally ANY message you want to get across is competing with hundreds of other messages. What you now need to learn is more than just public speaking - it's about getting your message across with confidence, sending it clearly and increasing the chances of getting it heard by other people.

To develop your skills, go and listen to other speakers – they might not be "perfect" but there's always something to learn. I watch experts at evening networking events speak at least once a fortnight and regularly attend conferences and seminars. I've also listened to many after dinner speakers and comedians. When you watch them, learn from their content but also evaluate what they did well and what they could do even better, decide what you liked and what might work well with your own style - and what wouldn't match to your inner speaker.

Once you get going on your learning journey, you might decide to really stretch yourself by being on your feet in totally different situations from those you're used to. Maybe you can start combining speaking with a hobby or interest you've hidden under a bushel for a while. Remember, the more flexibility you have the better the presenter you'll be because you'll have more skills and abilities to share with the audience if the need arises. Here are a few things I've done - and I hope they help you to think about what might be fun for you:

- Join the local Toastmasters International speaking group (www. toastmasters.org/). This is a friendly speakers group who meet fortnightly and most towns have a group. My experience of them in the UK is that they're hot on feedback for everyone involved, with a supportive environment and a well-structured development path. They also encourage you to do a few minutes' talk on a surprise topic, which gives you great experience. There are some rules that I'd call conservative but if you take the experience for what it is you really can grow and develop and get plenty of time on your feet practising. In addition, they're extremely cost effective

- Do a comedy course – again, these are usually pretty cost effective and a good opportunity to push your comfort boundaries. It doesn't mean you need to want to become a comedian, but it might help you to get in touch with the fun side of your inner speaker! Initially I started comedy so I could empathise with the monkeys – it was my version of terrified. Now stand-up is something I enjoy doing, but due to time commitments I don't want to "do the comedy circuit". I created a great compromise that works for me at the moment, which is to do charity gigs only. It means the audience is mostly friendly and forgiving, it's all for a good cause and often to a more appropriate target audience than I'd find in a comedy club in London. I currently use it to practise and experience learning lines word for word and for testing out new material each time. The current routine I'm working on is called "I Love Monkeys!" I'll put the link to the YouTube clip on my website if you are interested in checking it out and having a laugh – either with me or at me! (Search for" I Love Monkeys stand-up comedy" on www.deeclayton.com)

- Start acting or performing - many of the skills and techniques you learn can be transferred into your speaking skills and it certainly builds your confidence. I've done some acting in "murder mystery" dinners lately because I realised I'd never ever done any acting! The audience is having dinner with you and you're in character at the table, acting out scenes between courses! You really have to think on your feet because you never know what questions they might ask and you need to work with the other actors to support the story you just gave! All great learnings for me and more experience! By the way, that doesn't mean when you're presenting you pretend to be someone else – ALWAYS be yourself! I believe the only way you can be a great, natural and professional presenter is to be yourself, because then you can never be "found out" or" uncovered". They can only ever find *you*. Whether they like you or not – that's another matter! But you certainly have more chance of people liking you and being able to connect with you and your message if they can see you're being genuine.

Help others

Finally many self-development experts support the belief that helping others is a great way to embed learning and help yourself. Teaching or helping others gives you a different perspective – no longer are you the presenter or the audience;

you've become the teacher! Viewing things from another angle gives you the opportunity to see and learn many new things. Also, helping others is very rewarding and you never know how much you've changed someone's life for the better. Of course, I often stay in touch with my one to one mentoring clients and I hear of their successes. I hear about the impact of my teachings after a presentation less often - nevertheless, I'm increasingly finding that people who've seen me talk a few times come up and say, "You know that thing you said a year ago? It made a huge difference to me!". Sometimes it might have only been one sentence or an answer to their question - but whatever it was it was the right thing for them and drove them forward to succeed. You too can help others and, because success works on a spiral basis, even a little bit of help might be enough to set someone else off on that upward spiral of success.

So if someone close to you tells you they're scared of presenting, please buy them this book and offer to be their buddy. They might need time to come round to the idea, so encourage them gently and not only will you be helping them but you'll also be helping yourself to embed the learnings and continually tame mini monkeys who might pop up from time to time as you push yourself further along the speaker's journey.

Also let's help one another by sharing our successes and stories in the public speaking monkey community on line. Post up questions (because other people might have them to) and I'll do my best to answer them in a timely manner. Better still, get up and speak about your product, service, passion or successes. Inspire other people to start their speaker's journey and achieve their dreams. The best thing you can do to help others is to be a shining example, to your colleagues, your family, your children and your community.

"Be the change you want to see in the world."

Mahatma Gandhi

Next steps

Take action ASAP

Getting up to talk is the final piece in the puzzle. After all that's what it's all about. It's a bit like learning to use a new programme on your computer. No matter how many books you read or DVDs you watch - at some point you just need to turn the computer on and start using the system. It may not flow smoothly the first time and you might notice there are plenty of ways to improve, but the only way you get to learn to be good is to get on and start using the things you've learnt.

My advice to you is to get up and practise so your new learnings become embedded in your body's muscles. **Get on your feet and speak to an audience as soon and as often as possible.** It might be a short talk at a friendly gathering or a formal networking group. Even if you don't think you can find an excuse - invite some friends round and give a practice presentation to them. Or stand up and speak at a committee meeting or school PTA, perhaps give your team a five-minute update or visit a local speaking club. Anything at all that gets you up and speaking in front of others is essential.

Follow the techniques I've recommended, not only for monkey taming but for the practical parts too. Always prepare - even if you only have a short time span, still prepare using 4MAT®. Practise and save time by working on only the bits you need to. The tips have worked for me and for my clients and I know they will for

> **Get on your feet and speak to an audience as soon and as often as possible**

you. All you need to do is put in the effort to follow a new approach and then see it working for you. Keep using the approach and notice how much easier it becomes every time.

Some people ask me how they should feel after presenting and of course that's personal to you, but when people speak and once they get into the flow they often complete their presentation and are left totally unaware of where the time went. They say they weren't consciously thinking about the presentation – they did all that in the preparation and practice stages. When they delivered the presentation they were just being themselves and being 100% in the moment, allowing their thoughts and beliefs to inspire and captivate the audience.

It's a bit like driving down the motorway without realising all those junctions you passed until it's time for your turning. You've arrived there safely and it's OK if you don't remember it all - just knowing the audience thought it was good is enough. One last tip - it's good to record all your talks so then when you're in the zone and can't remember how good you were, you can go back and consciously hear what went well so you can repeat it and learn from it, giving yourself the feedback sandwich based on reality now, not monkey mutterings!

As you travel your speaker's journey, no matter where you started, remember it is a journey. There is no start or finish where one day you become a natural speaker; it's all a journey, so you might as well enjoy it! Pick one area at a time for improvement and gain constructive feedback on that area. Keep an open and positive mindset, learning from others who are skilled in their craft.

I wonder if you remember way back at the beginning when I mentioned the three steps to speaking excellence that have worked for so many people to date? Well, congratulations on completing the first step of taming your monkeys! This is the least easy step of all because it required that leap of faith, a belief that by doing things in a different way your results will change. And they have - well done!

Plenty of people stop after this step. They've achieved their goal of being a fear-free public speaker and that's great and they go on to be good speakers. Others, when they lose their fear, realise that they have a message they need to share. They decide to set themselves some big goals around being an excellent, effective and an enjoyable speaker to listen to or finding their inner speaker and uncovering their purpose. There are many ways to progress your journey, and I hope I can remain a part of it. Visit the website www.DeeClayton.com where there's plenty of free advice and discussions and I'll see you there, but for now at this stage of the journey, this is where I leave you and look forward to hearing all about your success stories and achievements soon.

Every success.

Dee